Gambling Addiction

A complete guide to survival, treatment, and recovery from gambling addiction and problem gambling

Kurt Dahl

Published by PDKYT Publishing

www.gamblingaddictionbook.com
Inquiries to: pdkyt2020@gmail.com

ISBN 9798681471486

First edition

Cover Art by Agnesa Mahalla, Kosovo

Other books by Kurt Dahl:
Fiction:

The Eden Proposition

This is the defining book on what might actually be going on in our exploding pandemic world. This book was first published 11 years ago and predicts the pandemic that we are seeing now, and more importantly, the startling, and horrifying conclusion that could possibly lie ahead

An American Famine

An American Famine combines the realism of our most knowledgeable pundits on sustainability along with a vivid fictional descent into chaos and anarchy. It aims to be the Rosetta Stone for those people who are concerned about our future but are unsure about the outcome - it translates their vague fears into a clear and potent picture of the danger ahead.

This book is dedicated to:

William Grant Van Dyke.

Without his abiding friendship, guidance, and generous support over the past two decades this book would never have been written.

Table of Contents

Foreword

Insidious: in an inconspicuous or seemingly harmless way, but actually with grave effect.

Gambling Disorder (a.k.a. compulsive gambling or gambling addiction) is an insidious disease. It is increasing dramatically in the United States and around the world. Only a few decades ago, the only places to gamble legally in the U.S. were Las Vegas, Atlantic City, or the racetrack. Today, there are large casinos in virtually every state – over a thousand full-scale casinos with over a million slot machines. Not only are gambling opportunities available within a short driving distance, they are available in our homes and in our hands through mobile devices.

One is only a Google search away from reading reports from gambling commissions around the world to realize that over half of those who gambled, used mobile devices, with slot type of gaming being steadily popular as the boundaries between social casino gaming and commercial gambling become increasingly blurred. With this sudden exponential increase in access comes the rapid and significant increase in addicted gamblers.

"Heroin could no longer numb my pain, but slots could."

Regardless of the type of gambling, gambling addiction can lead to suicide. The emphasis of Mr. Dahl's book is on slot machine gambling. Slot machines are called the "crack-cocaine" of gambling for a reason. The near-miss and other design features along with the ability to spend more time on devices (games) without interruption contributes to slots being king in the gambling word in terms of profit but also for addiction potential. The above profound statement, made by a person experiencing a gambling disorder and issues of unresolved grief, is all the heartbreaking proof you need.

Problem gambling is a public health issue that can have serious consequences for all involved. As there continues to be increased access to all forms of gambling across the United States through state-sanctioned gambling, as well as technology advances prompting on-line gambling, and changes in legislation legalizing many forms of gambling that were previously unavailable, adults and in particular youth, are likely to continue to experience negative consequences of problem gambling.

As reported by the National Council on Problem Gambling, one in five individuals experiencing a gambling disorder will attempt suicide, a rate many times higher than any other addiction. An explosion of newly addicted gamblers could result in a disturbing and dramatic increase in gambling related suicides. We have already seen it with slot machines over the past couple of decades. This sad and dangerous upward trend will continue and accelerate for years to come. Thousands of lives are lost every year. Families are shattered. The issue of suicide by people who have lost everything to gambling must be addressed and ultimately dealt with in a way that has a positive impact.

Mr. Dahl's book is relevant, particularly in today's changing world. Many people find themselves gambling to escape the stressors they have encountered in life. The COVID-19 pandemic has brought about isolation, grief, trauma, boredom, and financial problems; all risk factors associated with problem gambling.

Starting with the original title – *Please Don't Kill Yourself Today (You Can Always Do It Tomorrow)* – and ending with the appendix which makes a reasonable calculation of annual suicides by problem gamblers, Mr. Dahl's book is a breakthrough in bringing gambling-related suicides to the forefront of our thinking about gambling addiction.

Everyone experiencing a gambling problem should read this book. More than half of the book outlines ways to help with gambling treatment and recovery. But I also want to offer advice to all the counselors and trained professionals that read this book.

First, understand that problem gamblers are extremely secretive about their gambling, in large part due to feelings of shame. If you are a mental health provider, or an addictions counselor, it is very likely that you are already seeing someone who has been negatively impacted by someone's gambling, if not their own. Have the conversation and screen for problem gambling. There are high rates of co-occurring conditions in people experiencing problem gambling. Depression and alcohol use disorder are two of the most common.

Second, if you are treating someone for their gambling problem, continue to assess for and discuss suicidal ideation with them. Since you are reading this book right now, you will soon learn Mr. Dahl's specific plan for preventing the gambler from committing suicide. Please discuss and work that plan with your client. It might just save their life.

I cannot emphasize enough how important this book is to every addiction counselor and mental health professional. Please spread the word to all your colleagues. Let's save lives!

Sheryl Anderson

Project Turnabout's Vanguard Center for Gambling Recovery

Introduction

This book takes a new approach to confronting the epidemic of suicides that have resulted from the extraordinary increase in gambling addiction sweeping our nation and the world. To date, all books on this topic have been based on quitting gambling. In contrast, this book is focused on preventing the despairing gambler from committing suicide. The twelve-step program has no benefit to a dead person. In order to recover, the addict must stay alive.

In this book, I will focus on slot machine addiction. That is my addiction, and that is what I know. Other forms of gambling addiction have high rates of suicides as well, and I believe that those addicts will also benefit from this book.

Slot machine addiction is like a computer virus. Numerous studies have shown that the machines literally reprogram your brain by altering the chemical balance of the reward system. As with a computer virus, once the slot machine virus has infected your brain it is very hard to dislodge. Most people with this addiction have attempted multiple times to eliminate it and they have failed. Each failure leads to deeper despair and hopelessness. Often, when a computer virus appears impossible to eliminate, the only guaranteed solution is to get rid of the computer. So too with the slot machine addict – eventually suicide emerges as the only solution to their seemingly inescapable addiction.

But the truth about computer viruses is that they can be fixed. The right person with the right knowledge and the right tools can bring the computer back to life. It's not easy, but it can be done. This is also the truth about slot machine addiction. Eventually, with the right approach and the right help, slot machine addiction can be overcome. Many have done it. The despairing addict needs to know this and to believe this. There is hope.

I am not a therapist, psychologist, or a mental health professional of any kind. I am simply a slot machine addict who has been fighting to get the monkey off my back for 18 years. I've been to every kind of treatment available, and yet I continue to fight the good fight.

This is what I believe: Slot machine addicts don't commit suicide because they have lost all their money, or feel guilt, or shame, or feel weak, or are tired of lying. They commit suicide when they finally conclude that they will never be able to quit gambling - that no amount of will power or treatment will ever help them to stop. They commit suicide when they finally decide that all hope is gone.

Try this thought experiment. An addict is only minutes away from committing suicide. She is about to step on the chair and put the rope around her neck. A Fairy Godmother appears and offers her a pill that will absolutely eliminate her addiction; she will never gamble or *ever want to* gamble again. The Godmother says to her, "This is your choice: step on the chair and end your life, or simply take this pill".

Of course, she will choose the pill. Understand that the only thing that has changed in her life is that she knows that she will never gamble again. All the other elements and consequences of her addiction remain. She will choose to stay alive even though she is still broke, and her guilt and the shame are all still present. She will choose to live because she knows that she can rebuild her life as long as she never gambles again.

Unfortunately, there is no pill. However, there is the assurance that it is possible for all slot machine addicts to stop playing. There is no one path to that outcome. Everyone is different. The paths are long and hard and full of failure. But if you keep trying, you can get there. Something will eventually work. Know that, stay alive, and don't give up.

My hope is that this book will help the addict think differently about the process of recovery, and that it will help the addict see that the knowledge gained from each failure will become a building block on the path to recovery, and not just another tumble down the black hole of despair. The idea is to keep learning, keep trying, and don't give up. Don't ever give up.

So... please don't kill yourself today (you can always do it tomorrow).

How to use this book:

My hope is that the addicted gambler will read this book and heed the advice to prepare for that moment, after a relapse, that moment of walking away from the casino when hopelessness and despair overwhelms them. That moment when suicide becomes the only way out.

The detailed, specific, and comprehensive preparation outlined in the first few chapters of this book is designed to intervene and derail the end stage suicidal process. At that existential moment, the Cliff Notes message of this book is this: Just wait, step back, keep trying, and please don't kill yourself today.

Okay then. Good. Read the first half of the book, understand and accept the advice to prepare seriously, then swallow your pride, get off your butt and DO the actual work! If you do, you probably won't kill yourself today. That's a good thing. *But* what about tomorrow?

In Gamblers Anonymous (GA) meetings and from some therapists it is commonly stated that "Compulsive gambling is a progressive disease that is incurable and often ends in death". That's not an encouraging statement. My guess is that the original purpose was to jolt those people who were not entirely convinced that their gambling addiction was even a disease out of their denial, and to convince them that they had a serious problem that needed to be dealt with vigorously.

I do agree that slot machine addiction is a progressive disease, both in the amount of time spent doing it and the size of the bets. I also agree that it often results in death – that is what this book is about. But I don't agree that it is incurable.

Compulsive gambling is curable - thousands have done it. By curable, I mean that the compulsive slot machine player no longer plays slots. This doesn't mean that they don't have a desire to, just that they don't act on that desire. That is the goal after all - to not waste time and money sitting on that stupid stool endlessly pushing that stupid button.

The first half of this book "Saving Lives" offers ideas about how to prepare to derail that critical moment when the impulsive gambler decides to commit suicide. I am convinced that if the preparation recommended in this book is successfully accomplished, that the existential moment will pass with a decision to live rather than die.

As I stated earlier, it is my contention that the despairing gambler arrives at that terrifying moment of decision because they have lost all hope of being able to quit gambling. But, of course, escaping that moment by staying alive does not lead to restoring hope, it merely provides the *opportunity* to restore hope. This is where the second half of this book "Restoring Hope" steps in. There I explain and summarize, to the best of my knowledge, the many therapies available to treat gambling addiction.

In my research, I have not come across any book or article that in one place examines all the various treatments for dealing with a gambling addiction. Since many books and articles are written by professional therapists or academics, they usually deal with the specific therapy that they teach. They write what they know. What I know, however, is that there are a variety of approaches - from GA to inpatient programs, from Cognitive Behavioral Therapy (CBT) to mindfulness, from financial controls to voluntary exclusion, and many other effective methods that can help get that monkey off of your back.

First, you must understand and accept that there is always hope that you can stop gambling. Then read about all the choices and try as many as you want. If GA doesn't work, try mindfulness. If CBT doesn't work, try DBT. Combine them - do GA, financial controls and mindfulness. Try them all. Just keep trying. If you do, you will find the right path. You will succeed.

Thank you for reading this book. It is my sincere belief that it will save your life, restore your hope, and put you on the path of a gambling free life.

PART ONE

Saving Lives

Chapter 1

Let's talk about suicide

"The bravest thing I ever did was continuing my life when I wanted to die."
Juliette Lewis

A little past 4 on a January morning in 2005, I dragged myself out of a casino north of Seattle after twelve straight hours on a slot machine, pushing the play button as fast as I could until I had lost all my money. I got into my truck and sat in the parking lot for several minutes. I finally decided that I would take the one path that absolutely guaranteed I would never gamble again.

I unclipped my seatbelt, pulled out onto the I-5 freeway, and pushed the accelerator of my ten-year old F-150 to the floor. To my surprise within a minute or two I was doing 110 mph. My goal was to find a solid concrete bridge abutment and plow into it head-on.

I figured that my impending death would not be identified as a gambling-related suicide. This would spare my children the stigma and the conflicted emotions. I also figured that the concrete collision would be a one-car accident involving no one else. I could then make my final exit with very little attention. It would simply be regarded as a bit of bad luck on the highway.

What is normally a 40-minute drive to Seattle took me only 17 minutes. The highway department had done their job perfectly, protecting all hard surfaces with strong guardrails. There were simply no abutments that I could hit. I thought about flipping the truck over but decided I couldn't be sure that it would not involve another car, or that it would absolutely kill me. Or perhaps I was just not ready to finish the job. For those 17 minutes I wasn't really thinking. I do remember yelling a lot, and I did need to concentrate in order to stay on the road in that old pickup doing 110. Fortunately, for those 17 minutes there were apparently no State Patrol vehicles on that section of I-5.

This true story is not intended to elicit empathy or gain credibility with other despairing addicted gamblers. Instead, it is intended to show how difficult it is to know how many gambling suicides occur every year. Had I been successful in smashing into an abutment and killing myself, my death would not have been listed as a suicide, and certainly not as a gambling related suicide. I did have several beers that night so it likely would have gone down as drunk driving.

According to the Centers for Disease Control (CDC), suicides in general are underreported by as much as 50% (I believe this is a conservative number). In most states a coroner or medical examiner must certify on the death certificate that the death was a suicide. The certifiers are often hesitant to indicate suicide for various reasons. See the quote below from the CDC:

"The determination of suicide requires that the death be established as both self-inflicted and intentional. For most certifiers, establishing intentionality is the most difficult criterion. A coroner or medical examiner who suspects suicide may be reluctant to impose social stigma, guilt, and loss of insurance benefits on the victim's family. Since many certifiers lack explicit criteria for assessing suicidal intent, they might search for a narrower range of evidence concerning intent. Thus, a certifier might conclude that a death was not a suicide because information proving intent was not collected. However, absence of evidence of intent is not evidence of absence of intent. Some certifiers require a suicide note to certify a death as suicide. Yet, only about one third of persons who commit suicide leave such notes."
CDC

Think of a coroner facing the prospect of denying a family the proceeds of the victim's life insurance policy, especially if that person's income supported the family. Often the addicted gambler *commits suicide* expressly to provide their family with life insurance proceeds in order to pay off the gambling debt. If there is any possible doubt that it was a suicide, they will likely call the cause of death "undetermined" and therefore allow the family to collect the insurance payout.

If suicide in general is significantly underreported, documenting a suicide as gambling-related is orders of magnitude more difficult. As you well know, gambling addicts are very secretive. Even if a gambler had written a suicide note, and even if gambling was the real cause of their suicide, they probably would not say so. They would want to spare their loved ones the anguish and confusion - just as I had planned to do.

Gambling suicides are also frequently impulsive. My attempt to find a concrete wall to splatter myself on is, unfortunately, quite common for compulsive gamblers. I've had many conversations with other gamblers who tell the same story - looking for something to smack into on the way home from the bad beat at the casino.

Through my research, it appears to me that somewhere around 20,000 people died in 2019 in single car, single occupant accidents. And since it is very hard to determine whether these accidents were self-inflicted, my guess is that close to none of those 20,000 were reported as suicides. I'd like to know how many of these single-car fatalities occurred within 20 miles of a casino. I have no doubt that many of these deaths were despairing gamblers who found their concrete final moment.

For all the reasons stated above, there is simply no reliable data telling us how many gambling related suicides occur each year. Any attempt, by anyone, to propose an estimate of total annual gambling related suicides is little more than a guessing game.

I'll play that game now.

Below is a graph (from Wikipedia) of total reported suicides in the United States from all causes for the years 1981 through 2016.

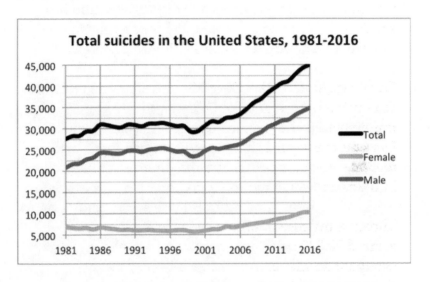

(Top line is total suicides, middle line is male suicides, bottom line is female suicides)

The upward trend in annual suicides continued into 2019 with approximately 50,000 suicides.

Anecdotal evidence (and some small surveys) indicate that gambling addicts have far more suicidal thoughts and attempts than other at-risk groups such as drug and alcohol abusers. Some claim that ratio is as much as five times to fifteen times higher than those groups.

Others who have attempted to estimate gambling related suicides have decided that an estimate of 5,000 to 10,000 might be in the ballpark. However, due to the massive underreporting of gambling as the reason for suicide, along with the certainty that suicides in general are severely underreported, and considering that there is a rapidly emerging epidemic of problem gambling - my guess is that actual annual gambling related suicides in the U.S. could be as high as 20,000 per year.

To put this into perspective, there were 39,733 total gun deaths in the U.S. in 2017. Of those 14,542 were homicides, and 23,854 were suicides. Total homicides from all causes in 2017 were 19,510, and total suicides were 47,173. I am proposing that there are roughly as many suicides related to gambling addiction every year as there are total homicides. (Please see appendix two for a more detailed look at how I arrived at these numbers).

Take another look at that graph. Do you see a dramatic rising trend starting in the year 2000 and continuing until today? I became addicted to slot machines in that year. During that year the first generation of computer-controlled slot machines were just beginning to emerge. These new slot machines were computer controlled (i.e. no longer random) and were designed to hook the player into continuous play in order to maximize the casino's return.

Over the next two decades, these machines have become more and more adept at achieving that goal. Coupled with the dramatic increase in the number of casinos and the rapidly increasing number of slot machines available across the country during the last two decades, the epidemic of slot machine addiction took off in the year 2000 and is now in full bloom. Look at the graph again, I will claim that the upward trend in suicides since the year 2000 is in good part a result of the increasing number of suicides that could be directly attributed to slot machine addiction.

(Once again, let me disclaim: There are no studies, or really any good data sets, to prove my assertions (or anyone's assertions) about the root causes of suicides. But since I am not a professor of statistics, or a professional therapist, or a medical professional at the CDC, I can pretty much say anything I want without consequence. I have no professional reputation to protect. My freedom to speculate could be good thing or a bad thing - you can decide.)

It is also important to understand that problem gambler's suicides are different. The therapeutic community has established that those with a gambling problem are impulsive. They are deficient in impulse control compared to the general public. In fact, in the 1980's, the DSM (2) identified compulsive gambling for the first time as a mental disorder and placed it in the category of Impulse-Control disorders. It wasn't until the latest version of the DSM (DSM-5 that came out in 2013) that compulsive gambling was moved to the addiction section.

There is a strong consensus that problem gamblers are impulsive, and I would suggest that slot machine addicts are even more impulsive than other gamblers. Problem gamblers are also risk takers - obviously, gambling is a risk-taking venture. And since it is also generally accepted that impulse control problems, and risk-taking behaviors, are characteristics that can contribute to a potential suicide, problem gamblers are at a substantially higher risk for suicide than the general public.

As I mentioned in the introduction, I believe the suicide tipping point for problem gamblers happens when they conclude that they can never stop. That no amount of willpower and no version of treatment will ever be effective. This belief destroys hope. And, once hope is gone, they decide that they should go too.

How does this final descent into hopelessness occur? Clearly, for the slot machine addict, it comes about immediately after long hours at a casino spent pushing the button on the slot machine that ends in significant and irrecoverable losses. At that point, their head is spinning. Their brain is misfiring. They are tired and despairing. It is one short step to utter hopelessness. Quite literally, the next few minutes could determine whether they live or die.

Slot machine gamblers are far less prepared to face this existential moment of despair than are other potential suicides. Another trait that gamblers possess is optimism. All gambling episodes begin with the positive belief that this time they just might win. Optimists generally don't prepare themselves to consider suicide. On the day that I walked into the casino, on that day that led to my high-speed search for a concrete wall, I was happy, excited, looking forward to playing the slots. As I walked into the casino, committing suicide was the very last thing on my mind. Yet, twelve hours later, it was the only thing on my mind.

This is the moment of truth for this book. The next few chapters are intended to instruct the problem gambler on how to prepare for that existential event. That moment when they descend into hopelessness at the end of a disastrous gambling session. That critical moment when they might decide to kill themselves.

Really? Is that even possible? Can someone actually prepare for such an unexpected, unanticipated, overwhelmingly emotional experience such as the decision to commit suicide? The answer is yes, of course. The essential idea of this book is that the problem gambler must anticipate, even expect, that in the course of their quest to stop gambling they will at some point face that horrible decision. That at some point they will seriously consider killing themselves.

The critical proposal of this book is that the problem gambler needs to prepare for that frightening moment *well before it happens*. They need to prepare at a time when they are not gambling, at a time when they are still hopeful that they can recover, at a time when the addict is thinking clearly, motivated to stop, and willing to consider actions to help themselves recover.

The first step in that preparation is to simply accept the fact that they might relapse. This is not intended to plan for or give an excuse to relapse. It is instead an acceptance of the fact that before they will be free of their gambling problem for good, the odds are that they will relapse. Studies have shown a very high level of relapse for problem gamblers, some as high as an 80% chance of relapse following their first attempt to stop. Relapse is a completely expected event for the compulsive gambler.

Standard belief among therapists and gambling addiction professionals is that each relapse triggers a steeper fall into addiction, that each relapse generally exhibits more intense gambling behavior, bigger bets, and less control. Each relapse reinforces hopelessness by providing hard evidence that the addict will not be able to quit. It gives credence to the gambling addict's belief that they will never fix the problem, and then, in total hopelessness, it significantly raises the potential of suicidal thoughts and actions.

Perhaps it seems cruel, or counter-productive, to ask a recovering addict who is currently not gambling to consider that they might relapse. It could even be considered dangerous to ask a recovering addict to accept the fact that not only might they relapse, but that they may also consider suicide or even kill themselves. Some might say that this idea could be responsible for planting a thought that might become disastrous.

The benefits of talking and thinking about a potential suicide far outweigh the misconceived concept that "suggestion" will lead to a dangerous outcome. Suicidal thoughts need to be discussed. They need to be brought into the light and understood. I've seen eight different therapists in the course of my quest to stop gambling, and even these professionals never brought up the topic of suicide. They never asked if I was thinking about it.

Estimates indicate that there are between 3 to 8 million problem gamblers in the United states right now. I think it's more. I'm guessing that the people making the count do not go to a casino at 11:00pm on a Tuesday night and see just how many people are sitting at a machine in the standard heads-down, uber-focused, addicted gambler pose. The vast majority of those 8 million problem gamblers have not yet made the first step to recovery. They are still in denial. They want to keep gambling, so they convince themselves that they don't have a problem. This book is intended for those who have made the first step, for those who have accepted that they have a gambling problem and are trying, or thinking of trying, to stop. For those recovering gamblers, the concept of relapse has already become part of their thinking. After all, that is exactly the thing they are trying to avoid.

As every therapist and every book on addiction claims, the first step to recovery is to accept that you have a problem - to escape from denial. In some ways, for the problem gambler, this fact is obvious. They spend too much time at the casino, they have lost a lot of money, they feel shame and regret, and they are lying to their loved ones. These things are right in front of them, in plain view. When they are ready, acceptance of the problem is not that hard.

However, what I'm asking in this book is hard. To ask a recovering gambling addict to also escape denial about their potential for a future suicide is quite a leap. First, they believe (because they have to) that they will not relapse. So why should they plan for a relapse, much less a suicide? They also have probably not yet had any suicidal thoughts or attempts, so why would they even have to consider such an awful thing? The idea of preparation for a potential suicide just doesn't compute. It's not in their current reality.

But let's look at this backward for a moment. Let's consider all the compulsive gamblers who committed suicide last year (let's stipulate that the number was 10,000 people just to be on the conservative side). At one point in their descent into hopelessness each of these 10,000 people were attempting to recover - just like you. At one point they believed, as you do, that they were on the road to recovery. They believed that they were not going to relapse. And of course, many had never even come close to thinking about suicide - just like you. I will assert that this is true, at some point, for every one of them - all 10,000. But, *but, BUT*...they did relapse. They all did think about suicide. And then they all did kill themselves! All ten thousand. *They killed themselves.*

What do you think would have happened if all of them had followed the recommendations in this book? What if all of them had prepared for the possibility of relapse and the subsequent hopelessness and thoughts of suicide? If they had taken the few hours necessary to prepare thoughtfully and without denial, even though they were sure it would be a waste of time. What would have happened? Well...I think many of them would not have killed themselves. What percentage? Who knows. Still, many of them would have passed through that moment of decision and decided to live. What if only ten percent were saved? That is still a big number - that's a thousand people. I believe that if they had prepared as recommended in this book that more than half would have survived. Think of that.

Let me suggest one more way that gambling related suicides are different. The typical profile for a gambler's descent into hopelessness and possible suicide provides a unique opportunity for intervention in that process. The typical addicted gambler who is in recovery and not gambling, who is seeking help through G.A. or therapy, or even just using willpower to try to stop, is often in a positive frame of mind. At this point they can think clearly about their situation. This is not true for the many other addictions and mental illnesses (such as drug addiction, severe depression or schizophrenia) that lead to suicide.

The recovering gambler knows that relapse is the primary, if not the only thing, that will force a decent into a state of hopelessness and possible suicide. For the gambler, and specifically the addicted slot machine gambler, the relapse often begins in a positive state of mind. They gamble believing that this time they will win. Not only that, but this relapse event requires planning and a period of time before it begins. They must prepare, get money, and drive to a casino. That positive attitude, and especially that gap of time, gives the gambler a window of opportunity to prepare for the possible outcome of big losses and the resulting anger, depression, and hopelessness.

If you are a problem gambler reading this book, you are obviously looking for a way to stop. You have already escaped denial and accepted that you have a problem with gambling. I'm asking you to go a step further: Accept the fact that at some point in the future you might relapse (even though right now you have convinced yourself that you won't), and that the relapse might well cause you to consider suicide. Please do that right now - please accept the possibility that relapse, and thoughts of suicide might be in your future.

Now take the time to read the next few chapters that will tell you how to prepare, and more importantly, take the time to *actually do* the recommended steps. It will take only a few hours and will cost you virtually nothing. You must do this. It could save your life. Think of it like learning CPR, doing fire drills, learning the Heimlich maneuver, etc. Don't become one of those ten thousand people who might have been saved with proper preparation.

Please don't kill yourself today. Do the work right now. Choose to live.

Chapter 2

Please don't kill yourself today
(you can always do it tomorrow)

"Imagine how many suicide victims would still be with us, if only the right person said the right thing at the right time."
Wayne Gerard Trotman

If you are reading this chapter, it is likely that you have already accomplished the hardest part of this process. You have accepted the fact that at some point in the future you may relapse, and that after a bad relapse you might consider killing yourself. Congratulations! But is that enough to save your life? Now that you are aware of the possibility of relapse and suicide, will that keep you alive? Will you simply say "Self, I'm not going to commit suicide today", and then be safe from that awful outcome?

I wish it were that easy, but of course it is not. The overwhelming obstacle you will face after walking out of the casino, broke and despairing, is that your brain isn't working properly. Your brain is under the influence of a tidal wave of its own chemicals created by your gambling episode. Think of what you have just done to the three pounds of grey matter between your ears. You've spent 4, or 8, or 12 hours (or more) sitting still, frantically pushing a button thousands of times, and watching a screen of complex symbols and sounds flash into your senses every few seconds - *for hour upon hour upon hour*. The CIA could not come up with a better form of brain-altering torture - yet you do it willingly!

Why do you do that? Why do you subject yourself to that deliberate form of sensory overload? The answer is simple: you are addicted to it. Compulsive gambling is an addiction. All addictions share the same basic traits. Brain chemistry is altered and the reward system and the choice system in your brain is compromised to the extent that you do things that can harm you or kill you, even though at some level you know better. (See several references to a more detailed explanation of the altered brain chemistry of addiction at the end of this book).

Compulsive slot machine playing is so intense that it screws up your brain in other significant ways that we don't yet understand. The process of coming down from a heroin or alcohol high takes several hours or even days and the glide path is fairly steady and uniform. In stark contrast, the switch from being actively engaged in slot machine addiction, to the moment the money runs out and your emotions instantly switch from hopeful to failure and despair, occurs in a split second. It is a cliff with a ten-thousand-foot drop.

Slot machine addicts' brains are tuned to hope for, and even expect, that they will get the big reward (a big win) right down to their *very last spin*. Studies have indicated that the anticipation of a reward activates the dopamine cycle even more than an actual reward. One second the gambler is active in their addiction - the dopamine is flowing - and the next second the money is all gone and they can no longer anticipate a big reward. At that point they must get off the chair, step away from the machine, adjust their eyes to a larger field of vision, and then walk out the door in a trance, often into a dark and cold night.

The intensity and severity of that instantaneous transition from hopeful *to hopelessness* is so dramatic and dangerous that it has led to thousands of impulsive suicides.

Now that you know that you might relapse, and you know that after that relapse you might be feeling hopeless and prone to killing yourself, and you know that your brain isn't working right and will not protect you as thoughts of suicide well up, what can you do about it?

This is the big problem. Right now, for anyone reading this, it all seems so logical. "Okay" you say, "I get it. From now on I won't do that suicide thing." Good thinking, well done. Except, right now, while you are reading this, your brain is functioning normally. But when you walk out of that casino your brain is seriously screwed up. Your willpower is weakened, your risk-taking tendencies are increased, and your decision-making system is not functioning in a way that can protect you from harm. As you walk out of that casino your brain is trying to kill you (or at least not able to prevent you from killing yourself). This is why, last year alone, thousands of people, who were okay 8 or 12 hours earlier as they walked into the casino, are now dead.

This is why you must prepare now, while your brain is working properly. You can do things right now to prepare for that life or death moment. The primary goal of your preparation is for you to be able to walk out of the casino, get into your car, drive away, and totally *ignore what just happened*. Ignore the emotions, ignore the losses, ignore the despair, ignore the hopelessness - just drive on home as if nothing had happened.

What? *Really*? All of the therapists out there who are reading this paragraph are now going, "Whoa now buddy - we can't stuff these feelings away, we have to be honest about them, we have to deal with them or they will fester and hurt you down the line!". Yes, of course you must deal with them. Just not now. *Not now!*

I cannot emphasize enough how seriously your brain is compromised as you walk out of that casino. If you allow those strong emotions of loss, despair, and hopelessness to overwhelm you, your pre-frontal cortex (the part that regulates choice) will *not* protect you. As you sink into despair and ask if you should kill yourself, your brain might well go, "Yeah, sure, why not, I'm tired of this crap, I don't give a shit, just go ahead and do it." This is exactly what happened to those thousands of gamblers who impulsively killed themselves last year.

This is what happened to me immediately after walking out of the casino on that cold wet January night. It took me less than a minute to decide to kill myself. It was totally impulsive, with no consideration of the consequences to my friends, family, or even myself. My thinking consisted only of "screw this, screw the world, I don't want to do this anymore". But, fortunately, for whatever reason, I didn't die then. I survived that high-speed death trip home. Perhaps I survived so I could write this book.

Since then, I have relapsed too many times to count. I've had many bad losses that put me in dire situations. But I've never seriously considered suicide again after that desperate search for a concrete abutment. Shortly after that attempt I decided that I could not trust my thinking in the minutes and hours immediately after a bad session in the casino. I told myself that from that point on I wasn't allowed to have any negative thoughts about what I had just done for at least three days. I gave myself permission to ignore what just happened and ignore the consequences for a set period of time. Unwittingly, right then, I started the process of defining my personal recovery plan and preparing myself to avoid suicidal thoughts.

But enough about me; this is what you must do, and you must do it right now while you have a functioning brain.

Let's make this as simple as possible. Here is your four-step plan to stay alive:

1) Accept the fact that you might consider suicide after a bad relapse. Do that now.

2) In the minutes and hours after a relapse, give yourself permission to *ignore* the consequences of your relapse. Don't think about the lost money, or the consequences for family, work, or your own self-worth.

3) Wait four days before taking any direct action to address your gambling issues. Do not gamble during this time. Do not chase your losses. Do not "confess" to a significant other during this time. Do not rob a bank to cover your losses. Wait four days to make plans for recovery. Wait until your brain both is willing and able to help you make good decisions.

4) After four days, start to restore hope. Call the state helpline, get a recommendation for a therapist. In most cases the state will pay for therapy. Then go see the therapist. Find a GA meeting and start attending. Make thoughtful, careful plans about how to go about discussing your addiction with loved ones and how to deal with your financial problems. But most of all, understand that there is hope for you to live a life free of gambling. Thousands upon thousands have recovered. You can too.

The details come next. Good stuff.

Accept

As we all know, the first step in dealing with any addiction is to accept that you have it. This is the essential message of the first step in any twelve-step program. Obviously, since you are reading this book, you have gotten to the point where you recognize your gambling problem as something you need to address. You have accepted you have a problem with gambling.

Now accept three more things. Accept that you might, and probably will, relapse. Then accept that because of that relapse, you may think that you have no hope at all to stop gambling. And, finally, accept that in that moment of despair and confusion, that in that moment when hope disappears and you descend into utter hopelessness, that you may consider suicide as your only way out.

This is the hardest thing to do of all the ideas in this book. "Not me", you say, "I'm not the suicidal type. And, besides, I've quit gambling - this idea no longer applies to me". Unfortunately, lots of dead people every year had that same thought. Please remember that last year alone over ten thousand despairing, relapsing gamblers also thought it didn't apply to them. And then, somehow it did - unexpectedly, out of the blue - and now they are gone.

There is no legitimate reason not to do this. It doesn't cost anything, it doesn't take much effort, it won't do any harm, and it might just save your life. Once you have accepted all those things, you can prepare to successfully survive your existential moment.

Ignore

For you, the problem gambler, the time when you are most vulnerable to falling into total despair is immediately following a bad episode at the casino. What is the state of your mental condition as you walk out to the parking lot after pushing the button on the slot machine for too many hours, and reaching in your pocket one last time to see if you might have missed a dollar bill? What is really going on in your hyper-stimulated rapidly misfiring brain?

One obvious answer is that you are angry at the machines for beating you and angry at yourself for being so weak and falling for it one more time. A less obvious and more worrisome answer is that your basic ability to think rationally has been severely compromised. Those hours of fierce focus on the flashing screen have altered your brain.

This is why you need to ignore thinking about your recent losses, your inability to quit gambling, your desperate financial condition, your lies to loved ones, etc. These complicated and frightening topics cannot be rationally addressed by your misfiring brain. The mere focusing on these depressing topics can quickly drop you into the black hole of hopelessness and lead you to a final fatal decision that suicide is the only escape.

Instead of focusing on those dangerous topics with your compromised brain, give yourself permission to totally ignore what just happened. Defer any big ideas or decisions about your gambling, financial problems, or relationship problems for at least several days. Tell yourself in that dangerous moment that you have only one goal - and that is to stay alive. All the other plans and tough choices can safely wait a day or two.

This may seem easy, because naturally you don't want to think about those negative things. I'm not asking you to be in denial or overlook what just happened, but rather to *defer* thinking about the consequences for a long enough time for your brain to settle down. By temporarily avoiding these negative thoughts you are in fact doing the right thing, a good thing, and something that may keep you alive.

The idea of ignoring the consequences of a bad night at the casino seems reasonable right now. You are reading about it with a functioning brain. But what about that moment when you walk out of the casino desolate, freaked out, unable to think or concentrate? How can you come to that logical conclusion when your brain's logical conclusion section isn't working?

Solving this problem is where the real preparation takes place. You need to prepare yourself ahead of time to invoke the "ignore" process. The first step in that preparation begins now, well ahead of the relapse. Get out a three by six index card and write these thoughts on it:

1-800-273-8255 (National Suicide Prevention Hotline)

This will pass

My brain can't be trusted right now

I won't kill myself today (I can always do it tomorrow)

For now, I will IGNORE, IGNORE, IGNORE

1-800-273-8255

You may also write anything else on this card, or another card, or several others. These notes are messages to your future self. These are notes from a clear thinking you, to the brain scrambled you. Let's call these steering wheel cards. Maybe include a picture of your dog, or your favorite sports team (unless your hometown team is as bad as my homeboys, as that picture could cause serious depression). Create your own message, or take one of these:

1) Right now, this is the biggest fight I have ever been in. Think of how good it will feel when I win.

2) My future is filled with things that I have never experienced. I don't want to miss any of it.

3) Think of all the people who are about to die and what they would give for a second chance. I have that gift right now, right this second, a second chance - I'm going to take it!

4) Tomorrow the coffee will be magic, the air sweet. I will have survived!

5) Please God, if you will help me, I will promise to wait for it.

6) I have a lottery ticket in my pocket, I'm going to stick around to see if I won.

7) My mind is a powerful thing, I will fill it with positive thoughts and my life will start to change"

8) Gambling suicide person testimonial: "I wish I had read this book before I killed myself. Dead is such a permanent thing, and no fun."

9) Okay now dumbass - this is your problem - you take responsibility. Put on your big-boy pants and go to work. Stay alive, you can beat this.

10) Just start somewhere. Baby steps are still steps.

11) Think of a person who would actually be happy if you were dead. This is your opportunity to really piss them off.

12) When confronted with your gambling problem, a Zen master might say, "Have a cup of tea". Ponder that (seriously) for the next two days. It will come to you. Then reward yourself with a cup of tea.

13) Thousands of people have survived this addiction, have quit gambling, and have gone on to live purposeful lives. Stay alive, join them. It's a good group.

14) The wisdom of George W. Bush: "I know that humans and fish can co-exist peacefully".
If they can, so can you.

15) It is an absolute certainty that I have another chapter in my life. I need to stay alive to see how it comes out.

16) I have gone to the brink and then turned back. I have something powerful to build on. I will do that. I will turn back. I will build.

17) I really don't want to give up these things: Bill Murray movies, chocolate shakes, a perfect 4 iron to the green, a hot bath, brown paper packages wrapped up in string.

18) A Haiku:

I love my children
My death will hurt them
I will not do this

19) "I postpone death by living, by suffering, by error, by risking, by giving, by losing." - Anais Nin. So can you.

20) God could not be clearer: Thou shalt not kill. I am here to be alive, to survive. I will survive.

21) It's only money. It's not cancer. When I stop gambling, I can deal with money problems. It's only money.

22) Make up your own...

Give some thought now about that drive home from the casino. Load up an interesting podcast to listen to.

Or set your sights on the Dairy Queen three miles down the road where you can stop and get a caramel Frappuccino. But be careful about choosing music. Music can evoke strong emotions directly, so choose something safe like polkas or jazz flute. There are unlimited possibilities of things that could divert your possible descent into hopelessness, things that are personal to you. But just like the choice of music, be careful about things that may evoke emotions.

You can set your radio to something that will distract you, like sports talk radio or George Noory's Coast to Coast AM radio show (my personal favorite for late night driving). This description of Coast to Coast AM from his website: "Noory captivates program listeners with his discussions of paranormal phenomena, time travel, alien abductions, conspiracies and all things curious and unexplained". No danger here.

Put these steering wheel cards and things somewhere in your car. Put your radio station of choice on one of your preset buttons. Do this now. Don't wait. Then, if you relapse, and when you get to the casino, *before you go in*, take them out and put them on your seat or steering wheel. Set your radio to the station you have chosen, so that all you need to do is turn it on. Please don't avoid doing this because you might be embarrassed or think it's stupid. So what if it's stupid? You are at the casino. You are already being stupid. Not to mention, these simple stupid actions just might save your life.

Will that do the trick? Are you safe now? Unfortunately, no. A very hard part comes next. Let me ask you to go back to one of your worst experiences leaving the casino. Try to recall your emotional state. Were you angry, confused, despairing, depressed? As I've discussed, besides the obvious emotions, your brain chemistry was screwed up. You were not able to think properly. If you simply stumble out to your car, get in, and then see your card with instructions to ignore, ignore, ignore, you probably will grab the card, crumple it up, and throw it out the window with explicit instructions "to go ..."(you know the rest).

As you walk out of the casino, you are in no mood to do the rational thing. You must quickly do something to change that mood or you will be in danger. These next three steps are important and specific. They will work. Listen up.

Step 1) Immediately after you step through the exit of the casino and find yourself outside, stop. Then look at your hands for ten seconds. Examine them, turn them over, look at the lines, the freckles, the dirt under your fingernails or your chipped nail polish. Really focus, really study them, for ten full seconds. This is a surprisingly powerful mindfulness technique. It forces you to jump back into the present, thereby interrupting your thoughts about what just happened. More about this in later chapters. Do this. It works.

Step 2) Walk slowly to your car. Look up, breath as deeply and slowly as you can, concentrate on your breathing. This will help slow down your thinking.

Step 3) When you get to your car, just as you touch the door handle, say out loud "5 - 4 - 3 - 2 - 1 launch ignore". This is called a starting ritual. It was popularized by Mel Robbins in her book "The 5 Second Rule". It is intended to get you to start doing something that you want to avoid, even though it is something you need to do. Something like looking seriously at your prepared steering wheel card or cards. Something like making the conscious choice to ignore what just happened in the casino. 5 4 3 2 1 - ignore, ignore, ignore - tell yourself that. Do it - ignore. Then turn on George Noory and go get that caramel Frappuccino.

Now go one more extra mile to keep yourself alive (you are worth it!). Do this: practice these steps every time you go to the casino. You can even practice them when you go to the mall or go visit relatives. You can also use them to help with everyday problems. I use the looking-at-hands trick whenever I find myself indulging in a line of thinking that sends me down a dark path. It always works to get me back into the present. I use the 5 second rule to avoid procrastination - like avoiding writing this book. It's a simple way to make me turn off the cable news, get off the couch, and get back to my desk and start typing.

Here's an idea - the next time you decide to go gamble say this: "5 4 3 2 1 screw the casino, I want to keep my money". Who knows, that might work. Worth a try.

Ignore, ignore, ignore. It will save your life.

However, if none of these techniques worked, if you still got in the car angry and determined to do something drastic, call the suicide hotline number. Moments like this are why they are there. They want you to call. They will help you stay alive. If you have any doubts about your plans, **make that call.**

Wait

Several years ago, I knew a man, a friend of a friend who I would occasionally run into at the casino. He was clearly a heavy-duty compulsive slot machine player - maximum bets, completely focused, playing fast. He was also a family man, hardworking, very organized, a successful businessman. One night after losing a great deal of money, he came home and immediately (and impulsively) blurted out a confession to his wife (who did not know that he had a gambling problem). He confessed that he had lost all their savings and maxed out their credit cards - they were now completely broke.

His wife reacted as expected. She was upset in the extreme. She packed her bag and left him to go spend some time with a relative. So then...after she had abruptly left him, at that point he knew he had lost all their money and perhaps lost his wife as well, and that his children and his family would now find out his dirty little secret. He was alone with his darkest thoughts. It was simply too much to bear. When he didn't show up for work the next day a business associate found him in the garage, in his truck, with a hose from the exhaust stuck in a window. He was dead.

It is clear to me that he didn't kill himself because of that day's gambling experience - the bad beat, the big losses. After all, that had happened to him many, many times before. He killed himself as a result of his completely impulsive decision to confess to his wife! I'm guessing that if I could go find his cloud right now and interview him, asking if he thought that his impulsive confession was a good choice, he would say "no". He would say he should have thought it through more carefully.

Had he waited a few days to make such a momentous decision, he might still be alive. Had he waited a few days, until he was thinking more clearly, he might have called the problem gambling hotline, arranged to see a therapist, met with a therapist and created a plan to confess in a more controlled way and with a more positive approach. He might have arranged to turn over his credit cards to a trusted friend or advisor and figured out a short-term solution to his pressing financial problems. Instead he blurted out to his wife that he was a failure and that they were doomed.

The reason to wait a few days before considering any drastic and irreversible action is that your brain is still messed up. You can't trust your thinking. It may take several days for it to return to normal. Figuring out how you can face your gambling problem is a complex issue. There are many choices (see the chapters in the *Restoring Hope* section). Recovery is not something that you can will yourself to do in a day or two.

However, there is no need to wait when seeking help. Under the concept of "strike while the iron is hot" are things that your commitment-to-do may fade after day or two. Things like phoning the state helpline to find a therapist or finding and attending a GA meeting. And of course, if you find yourself still in despair and slipping farther down that black hole, immediately call the suicide helpline. Do not be embarrassed, that is why they exist, they want you to call.

Do wait on things like selling your truck, borrowing money from your brother-in-law, blurting out a confession, or embezzling money from your employer. Also, *without question*, wait on going back to the casino to chase your losses. Wait until your brain can help you avoid those irreversible mistakes.

But do *not* wait on your recovery. Rather than focusing on solving your financial problems, or dumping your guilt off on to someone else, use the energy from this period of extreme emotional confusion and distress to begin your recovery. Nothing will go farther to show your loved ones of your sincere intent to quit, and nothing will give a such a strong immediate boost to your personal mental health, than making that initial commitment to the long difficult journey of recovery!

To work through the many options available, you will probably need the help of a professional. Many people do not know that almost every state has trained gambling addiction therapists that are available to you at no cost. Simply call the state sponsored helpline and they can hook you up with someone locally. The gaming industry usually pays for these services. In my state, they are funded by unclaimed lottery tickets. More about these agencies in later chapters. This is one place you do not have to wait. If you know it is time for you to get help, either a therapist or an inpatient treatment program, do it now, before you chicken out.

If you followed these steps - Accept, Ignore, and Wait - you will survive the first few dangerous hours after your relapse. You will have survived! This is a good thing. Your survival not only gives you the opportunity to restore hope, it has already started you down that path. You have made a conscious decision to follow these specific steps designed to keep you alive. You wanted to live. This implies you want to find a way to stop gambling. You have now begun your recovery. You have earned the right to be positive that you can finish. Congratulate yourself, you are worth it!

Chapter 3

Detox

"Not until we are lost, do we begin to find ourselves."
Henry David Thoreau

"Turn your wounds into wisdom."
Oprah Winfrey

Most literature about suicide proposes the encouraging idea that if you can survive the first five minutes (or the first few hours, or the first twenty-four hours) of that moment when suicide seems like the only solution to your situation, then you probably will not kill yourself (at least for a while). Now, the fact that you are reading this sentence means that you did *not* kill yourself impulsively (perhaps this is because you read the last chapter and followed the provided post-relapse steps to survival). Regardless, you made it through an extremely dangerous moment. Excellent!

Yet, the next day all the depressing conditions that led you down that suicidal dead-end path still exist. Not only do those difficult issues remain, your brain is still not functioning properly. It is better than it was in those critical minutes after leaving the casino but is still not recovered from what you did to it only a few hours ago.

You wake up the next morning (if you slept at all), and once again the reality of your addiction overwhelms you. Yesterday, you lost a boatload of money. You screwed up your brain. You broke your commitment to never gamble again and you lied to your family and friends. If there were underlying problems that conspired to lead you to the casino to seek that costly escape in the first place (like serious depression or relationship problems), they are all still present. Clearly you are *not yet safe*. Ignoring these issues helped get you through the night, but that method of survival has a short shelf life. Now you must begin to face reality.

In the last chapter I suggested three steps to keep you alive: Accept, Ignore, and Wait. Now, starting with the first morning after a relapse and going on for several days to several weeks, you are in the "wait" stage. You are waiting to recover both your physical and mental health in order to make informed and positive decisions about your future. You need to wait because on that first morning (and for days to come) you are experiencing withdrawal from your intense gambling episode. Your brain is still not able to help you.

Drug and alcohol withdrawal symptoms and treatment are well understood, but very little is discussed about gambling withdrawal. Here is a commonly quoted list of the symptoms of drug and alcohol withdrawal: *nervousness or anxiety, insomnia, nausea, body discomfort, mood swings, poor sleep, lethargy, difficulty concentrating.* Do these symptoms look familiar to you?

After sitting hunched-over, eyes glued to that screen only inches away, pushing that button every three seconds and watching those complex configurations of colorful images flashing rhythmically, hypnotically, continuously, as fast as your mind can process, for hour upon hour upon hour, do you experience any of those symptoms the next day and the next several days? I know I do.

(Disclaimer: Unfortunately, once again, there is no good data available for the physical, or the emotional, or the brain chemistry aspect of withdrawal from a serious slot machine gambling episode. I can only relate my numerous experiences and those described to me by other addicted gamblers.)

As mentioned earlier, gambling addicts screw up their brains when playing slots intensely for many hours. It is my belief (standard disclaimer again, I'm not a scientist) that there are two somewhat separate processes involved that lead to different chemical imbalances in the brain. There is the well understood dopamine and serotonin reward cycle common to all forms of gambling, and then there is the sensory overload effect from hours of rapid screen flashing that is *specific* to slot machine gamblers.

This sensory overload is a massive stimulant to the brain. I believe (and there is some data that supports this) that it creates the same effect on the brain and the same symptoms as excessive *stimulant drug* usage (cocaine, meth, etc.). Therefore, it seems reasonable to believe that the withdrawal after a prolonged slot machine session is very similar to withdrawal from stimulant drug abuse.

Below is a passage from the drugabuse.com website (the helpline for American Addiction Centers Inc.):

"When a person stops using stimulants, they may experience a series of unpleasant withdrawal symptoms. Often, the physical and mental effects that present during detox and withdrawal resemble a near-opposite of the substance's primary effects. This means that stimulants, which normally provide feelings of enhanced mood and energy, have a withdrawal period that is characterized by feelings of depression, low energy, and lethargy.

In most cases, stimulant withdrawal does not produce life-threatening effects, but it can be difficult to cope with emotionally and physically...One of the biggest risks during stimulant withdrawal is intense depression that can be associated with suicidal ideation."

My experience with withdrawal from a long slot machine session tracks closely with what is commonly reported for stimulant drug withdrawal.

Below is a timeline for stimulant withdrawal (also from the Addiction Centers website).

Days 1-3

During the first 24 to 72 hours after the last use, former users begin to experience withdrawal symptoms, including fatigue, body aches, anxiety and a general feeling of unhappiness. They'll also start to crave the drug and may have trouble sleeping. Heavy users may also experience hallucinations, paranoia, and panic.

Days 4-10

Symptoms of stimulant withdrawal usually last about seven days. Towards the end of the week, most symptoms begin to subside, but drug cravings can become more intense. Extreme fatigue and severe depression may present.

Days 11-17

While most symptoms have begun to lessen, depression and insomnia may continue. For some, insomnia can lead to hypersomnia or excessive sleeping. Some users may also experience mood swings.

Okay, so what can you do with this information? For certain, you won't be able to go to a detox facility for slot machine withdrawal - there is no such place. Millions of compulsive slot machine gamblers go through this withdrawal event several times, maybe many times, every month. Yet there is no clearly defined treatment, no facility designed to help them, and no advice of value in the problem gambling literature.

There are approximately twenty thousand detox facilities for drug and alcohol abusers nationwide. I understand that withdrawal from all forms of chemical dependency is a more dangerous and difficult process than gambling withdrawal and that it often requires medical assistance. But still - twenty thousand to zero? I believe this: The weeks following a major slot machine relapse episode are dangerous for the compulsive gambler. I'm certain that a significant number of suicides have happened to compulsive gamblers who faced this withdrawal period without any help, or without even any *awareness* of what was happening to them.

What can you do after a relapse? Once again, I will offer advice based entirely on my own experiences. I would prefer instead to relay advice from therapists, or researchers, or the CDC, but unfortunately that information does not exist. We are on our own here.

For me, the first four days after a prolonged slot machine episode are the hardest. It goes like this. I do whatever it takes to get through the first night. I have been refining my relapse approach for fifteen years (after my one attempt at splattering myself), culminating in writing this book. The point is that you need to *do what is best for you* in those dangerous first few hours.

But enough about you, back to me. The next morning is somewhat of an anomaly. I generally feel pretty good, clear headed and a bit energetic. I believe the reason is that the dopamine, adrenalin, or other chemicals are still present in some form. They remain for a few hours, but only in the morning, then they go away and I crash hard in the afternoon. That first afternoon I can barely function. I'm exhausted and unable to focus. I usually stumble into bed early and sleep long hours that night. Then, the next two or three days are exactly as described in the timeline above.

My goal during this time is to take good care of myself. I try not to drink. I try to eat well and exercise. And though my energy levels are low, I try to accomplish as many small tasks as I can in order to experience something to feel good about. Simple tasks, chores I've been putting off: I clean my desk, trim my toenails, do my laundry, etc. Somehow these chores seem easier when I'm dragging. I can just put my head down and grind them out without much thought.

I know now that doing these little things and taking care of myself will get me through the week. Think of it this way: This healing process is very much the same as what you do when you have a bad cold or the flu. You take care of yourself, you get good sleep, you don't drink, you eat well, and then in just a week or two you are back to being yourself. If you do the same thing after a bad relapse, in a week or two you will also be back. Do whatever works for you to recover. Again, we are on our own here. You must create, and then execute, your own personal detox plan.

This is important. I'm not a person who has been susceptible to depression. But I can see how vulnerable, how defenseless, a person can be to suicidal thoughts when you combine depression with the dangerous symptoms of gambling withdrawal. If you suffer from depression, please prepare for this possibility. Have the National Suicide Prevention Hotline number in your phone or at least on a card. The number again - 800-273-8255. Put it in your phone right now. Do it. And promise yourself right now that if you feel yourself slipping into that dark pit, you will make the call. They want you to call, so do it.

Think about this now, if you are one of the countless slot machine addicts who gamble several times a week, you are constantly in a state of withdrawal. You never get out of it. The symptoms of lethargy, depression, difficult sleeping, and suicidal thoughts are now your everyday mental state. You may not be able to even remember what it is like to have your brain functioning normally. Perhaps after reading this book you can see how important it is to get your brain healthy again. Perhaps this will inspire you to quit for at least several weeks to see how good it feels to get back to normal. But if you are not able to quit, then consider an inpatient treatment option (see chapter 7). In addition to the intensive professional help provided, it will give you thirty days without the influence of the evil torture machines and allow you to clear your brain of all those dangerous chemical imbalances.

Thoughtful preparation, at a time when you are thinking clearly, is the best defense against suicidal thoughts. Keep that in mind as you create your own detox plan. Put the phone number in your phone. If you are simply aware of what lies ahead you can deal with it. Get through the week, be good to yourself. Know that the general feeling of tiredness and unhappiness will soon pass. You will feel better. Then, with a healthy mind, you can face the tough decisions and the hard work necessary for you to quit gambling and restore hope!

Then this happened, a true story

The morning, after I wrote the above paragraphs on gambling withdrawal, I was on my walk when, unexpectedly, out of nowhere, Mr. Addiction suddenly wedged his foot in the door of my brain. A minute later he burst through, opened his arms, smiled, and in his best Jack Nicholson voice announced: *I'm Back! Let's go!* It had been many months since I had gambled and at that moment my defenses were dormant. The guards were asleep. Without even offering a show of resistance, I immediately got in the car and drove south to where my favorite slot machine lived. I played for over eight hours at my usual furious pace until my available money was all gone and my brain was fried.

I'm writing about this relapse story now, six days after that episode, having just gone through all of the ugly phases of a serious relapse, *immediately after writing about it!* Ironic, I guess. Kind of circular. I'm not sure what to make of it. I'm not making this up. Though in retrospect, I've realized that I should have expected Mr. Addiction to show up and test me during this process. Writing this book is an intense experience. I'm writing about an addiction that I suffer from, I'm doing the research, I'm reading about it for hours, writing about it for hours, I should have expected that that extreme daily exposure to my addiction would eventually lead to strong urges to gamble. I should have been prepared! But I wasn't.

Hopefully, in a few months, after doing the research and writing the chapters in the second half of this book, I'll be much better able to understand and know how to disrespectfully decline those strong urges. You, on the other hand, can gain that knowledge right away. Read on.

The lesson here is to never get complacent, never let your guard down. Always be aware that Mr. Addiction is lurking, waiting for a weak moment to slip in and control you. You have all been there. You know how it happens. You get the urge, you find an excuse, and you go. Sometimes, it takes only seconds.

There is one more symptom of withdrawal that I learned about during this relapse. I think it might be important but I'm struggling for a way to describe it. In general, the withdrawal proceeded exactly as I had described above. I followed all the steps I discussed: I took good care of myself, I did a bunch of little chores I've been putting off, and I also tried to make notes about how I was feeling at every stage of the recovery (though I didn't have the ability on day-one to even be aware of how I was feeling). Day one is simple survival. But on days two through five I noticed that I couldn't generate any positive energy. I did what I could to feel better, but somehow there was a cap, a lid, a governor of sorts that wouldn't allow me to experience anything beyond just getting by.

Forgive me if this sounds new-agey, but I simply don't have the words to describe this. I'm a fan of Maslow, often cited as the first person to discuss positive psychology (as opposed to the early psychologists who focused on dysfunctional behaviors). One of Maslow's concepts is called a "peak experience". A peak experience is the flip side of a bad depression. Everything seems rosy, you feel terrific. I am fortunate in that I have had that feeling on occasion. More often (peak experiences are rare) I am also lucky to have what I call "little peaks". Hard to describe this, but it is something more than just being pleased with the day, or the work, or life in general. Maybe the best description is it's like being a little (naturally) high.

I think now, after reading about this brain chemistry stuff, that these little peaks are simply a minor surge of dopamine, generated by positive behaviors, or good news, or sunny days, or who knows what else. So, perhaps, after flooding your brain with dopamine as a result of your many-hour-slot-sit-down, that during the withdrawal period you are now suffering from a dopamine deficit. It may well be the cause of the multi-day lethargy and depression. Yet again an example of how slot machine addiction screws up your brain.

During this detox period it may be perhaps possible to raise the dopamine level in your brain naturally. These ideas are once again pure speculation. The brain chemistry of dopamine is extremely complex, and there is no simple way to measure its level in your brain. Still, it is speculated that vitamin D, magnesium, and omega-3 supplements may help raise dopamine, though there is no definitive proof. Those supplements are also good for many other things. Do your own research, and perhaps give them a try during your detox. Mood enhancing activities are also recommended for raising dopamine, things like exercise, meditation, prayer, music, etc. But please don't return to the casino in order to boost your dopamine. The resulting snap-back peaks and valleys will just get bigger and more dangerous.

Broken record time...the same advice for surviving the first few hours after a relapse applies to surviving the withdrawal period. Simply know that your brain is compromised, and please *prepare* for a difficult week. Then take care of yourself - like a bad cold, this too will pass.

Chapter 4

Do you want a future?

*"Though nobody can go back and make a new beginning,
anyone can start over and make a new ending."*
Chico Xavier

In the introduction I suggested the idea that if a fairy
godmother appeared at the exact moment when a
woman stepped onto a chair and slipped the noose
around her neck and offered her a pill that would
eliminate forever her gambling addiction (and even her
desire to gamble), that she would take the pill and step
down from the chair. She would choose to live, even
though she was still facing all the difficult and
depressing consequences of her gambling.

By reading this book, I hope that you have chosen to live, just like the woman on the chair. Unfortunately, you will also have to face all the consequences of your addiction. Those consequences can be significant. I've been in treatment with people who have robbed banks, who have stolen disability checks from vulnerable relatives, who have embezzled large amounts of money, who have taken valuable items from their parents to pawn. At some point in their recovery, most gambling addicts will finally have to pay the price for their destructive actions.

This book cannot help you with that process. You must do that heavy lifting yourself. What this book can do is to keep you alive, and then hopefully provide that pill that will stop you from gambling in the future. Know this: The first step that needs to happen before you can deal with your consequences is to *stop gambling*!

I can offer a few simple (and probably obvious) things to do about damage you may have done. If you have legal issues, consult a lawyer. If you can't afford one, try Legal Aid (Google "legal aid (and your state)"). If you have relationship issues, get a therapist as soon as you can. Remember that most states will pay for a therapist to help you deal with your addiction to gambling, and in that process, they can help you with all of your other issues as well. There are a variety of significant steps that you can take to resolve the consequences of your past actions. Even small steps are steps. But right now, your top priority, your first and most important step, is to stop gambling.

Once you stop gambling you can start to feel and think like a normal person (assuming there is such a thing). Your immediate financial situation will improve because you will no longer be stuffing $100 bills into those evil machines. The recovery process will take time, it will take sacrifices, it will take determination, and it will take very hard work. You can do it. Know that *you can* rebuild your life - many have.

What follows is the section called *Restoring Hope*. In this set of chapters I will summarize the many treatment options that can help you to stop gambling. There is a wide range of things you can try - from therapy to hypnosis, from mindfulness to financial controls. I've identified many of these different approaches with a chapter for each one of them.

In the following chapters I have summarized each of the individual concepts as best as I could, and I've provided references (see the references page at the end of the book) to help you learn how to put that approach into practice. More importantly, for each of these therapies/ideas/concepts, I have also tried to explain how they can be used to *specifically address gambling addiction*.

I know of no other place where you can find this kind of information. I've personally tried many of these ideas. I've worked with therapists on many of these ideas. I've explored these treatments with counselors in inpatient programs. And I've reviewed these chapters with several of the leading voices in the problem gambling treatment business. (Once again, I will disclaim. I'm not certified, or degreed, or recognized by any organization in the profession of problem gambling treatment. Though by now, you readers have perhaps concluded that I may know a few things about it.)

You, as a problem gambler who is trying to learn how to stop, will be well-served if you understand everything is available that might possibly help. Often, when you start working with a therapist, they will steer you to what they know. If their specialty is CBT, they will use CBT. I think that a very important component of your personal process of *restoring hope* is for you to be an active participant in your recovery. Please do not believe that someone else (or something else) will simply provide you with that magic pill. This is your circus.

I've read a lot of studies about problem gambling. They tend to bullet-point broad categories of us button-pushers. Things such as: sixty percent of us have other personality disorders (though, that may be true of the entire population), or twenty percent of us have attempted suicide. However, these studies can only survey those problem gamblers who have presented themselves for treatment - this is a self-selected group and a very small percentage of total problem gamblers. Since most problem gamblers are still in the closet, these generalizations should be regarded with some caution.

I don't believe there is a standard profile for problem slot machine gamblers. The ones I have met in treatment, and the countless others that I have encountered in the casino, are as varied as the entire population. And because of that, there is no cookie-cutter approach to treating slot machine addiction. There are many options, and each problem gambler needs to know what they are. That knowledge will empower them to choose what they think will work for them.

The therapists I've worked with (with one exception) have welcomed active participation by the patient. Please be active in your own treatment. Be informed. Read these next chapters. Try as many options as you think might help. Know that something *will* work. There is always hope! Don't ever give up.

PART TWO

Restoring Hope

Chapter 5

First Step - Therapy

Who looks outside, dreams; who looks inside, awakes
Carl Jung

"But why?" you ask, "Why should I see a therapist? Do they have the secret to curing my gambling addiction?" No, they don't. There is no secret, no magic pill that will overcome your addiction. But let me ask you this: Who are you able to talk to about your gambling? I already know the answer for 99% of you. The answer is *no one*. Am I right? Of course I'm right; gambling addiction is without any doubt the most secretive mental disorder that exists. Gamblers have so much shame and guilt that they cannot discuss their fears, the consequences, or even their suicidal thoughts with anyone. They are certain that no one they know will ever understand it, because they don't understand it themselves.

Not only do they avoid letting anyone know about their addiction, they can also easily get away with this extreme secrecy. They don't pass out, they don't smell bad, there are no urine tests that show they have recently gambled and for the most part they don't miss work. They gamble alone. Slot machine addiction is a solitary undertaking. It is not a social event like drinking or drug use. Slot machine addicts can gamble compulsively for years without family or friends even suspecting. In their solitude, the gambling addict lives a life completely alone with their fears, consequences, dark thoughts, and often, depression. They have no one to help, no one who will listen, no support at all. They are alone in this secret place - unless they seek help. I know. I've lived there for many years.

This is why gambling addicts need to get into therapy. They desperately need someone to talk to, someone who will not judge them, someone who is trained to listen to them share their pain and confusion. The fundamental benefit of therapy for a compulsive gambler is simply that - *someone to talk to.*

If you have not already sought a therapist, do it soon! Call your state's problem gambling hotline and arrange to see a therapist. In many cases the state will pay for these sessions. There is no need to feel guilty about accepting state money for your therapy, as it often comes from some aspect of the gambling industry. In my state it is funded by unclaimed lottery tickets! (If you already have a therapist, please read the rest of this chapter anyway, I think you will find valuable information about how therapy can work for you.)

Usually there is a sticker on every slot machine with the number to call. DO NOT go to the casino to get that number! Instead, go to the National Council on Problem Gambling (NCPG) website. This is the most important resource on the internet for problem gamblers. It has an abundance of information on everything you want to know about problem gambling and problem gambling treatment. On the website you will find a map of the United States and all you have to do is click on the state you are in (or in some cases, the state where you gamble) and it will give you the number to call for help.

NCPG	National Council on Problem Gambling

Website:	www.ncpgambling.org (note only one "g")
Call:	800-522-4700
Chat:	ncpgambling.org/chat
Text:	800-522-4700

If you are in one of the states where there is no direct support for gambling addiction therapy, perhaps your insurance will cover it. Medicaid may also be able to cover some of the cost of therapy. Below is a passage from the *2016 Survey of Problem Gambling Services across the United States* conducted for the National Council on Problem Gambling by Dr. Jeffery Marotta of Problem Gambling Services Inc.

"Key informants from 16 states indicated gambling disorder was covered under their Medicaid program (CA, CO, CT, DE, IA, MD, ME, NJ, NM, NV, NY, OH, OK, SC, VT, WI)."

This 2016 survey by Dr. Marotta is the best and most comprehensive national database of the available services for helping addicted gamblers. (It can be found on the NCPG website or google "2016 survey of problem gambling services"). Within its 162 pages (a PDF) is a list of each state's complete problem gambling services - what they provide, how they provide it, how much money it costs, and their annual budget.

But please, *even* if you are required to pay for it yourself, seriously consider finding and seeing a therapist. The money you will save by not shoving bills into that unholy slot in those unholy machines will more than cover the cost of your therapy.

According to federal Labor Department statistics, there are 552,000 certified therapists available in this country (this number appears to come from data around 2010, so there are probably many more currently). The certification process for designating a therapist as a compulsive gambling specialist is relatively new and not yet standardized. And while there are a few national organizations that recommend and certify training programs, it appears that many states have their own process for certification.

The state of Washington has around 100 therapists who are either certified or in the process of gaining certification. I would estimate that there are possibly 2,000 to 3,000 certified gambling therapists in the U.S. If you are working with your state gambling organization and they are financially supporting your therapy, they will likely recommend a certified therapist. A certified therapist has had training and likely has experience with other problem gamblers. They may also provide the opportunity join a group session that they conduct.

A certified therapist is certainly preferable. However, because the number of currently certified problem gambling therapists is small compared to all available therapists, do not hesitate to go to someone who is not certified. Don't assume that a therapist who is not certified does not have experience with gambling addiction. Even if they don't, they can learn with you and still be enormously helpful. It is possible that the state will pay for you to work with a non-gambling-certified therapist, perhaps someone you are already seeing or someone you know. Ask the therapist if they can apply to the state for the funds necessary to cover your sessions.

The mental health community in general is becoming increasing aware of problem gambling. Any good therapist will be able to have that desperately needed conversation about your gambling, regardless of specific problem gambling training. And, you have this book (you are reading this sentence after all!) that will guide you and help you (and your therapist) explore the many options available for your treatment.

The commonly quoted figure for gambling addicts having other treatable mental disorders is around 60 to 70 percent. In other words, most gambling addicts have other addictions, or suffer from depression, or are dealing with PTSD, or something else that is causing them difficulty. This, of course, is another important reason to seek treatment. You may well have other problems that you need to deal with. There is some good news in that statistic. Many insurance policies do not cover therapy for gambling addiction, but they might cover alcohol treatment or treatment for depression. So, seek help for those problems (if you think you have them), get a therapist, and then open the discussion about your concerns with your gambling.

A word of caution. I once attended a group therapy session with about four other problem gamblers. It was started by a certified gambling therapist, but she had moved to another state. The new therapist had group experience, but no problem gambling experience. The conversation during the session devolved into the telling of gambling "war stories" - i.e., big wins, what machines paid better, which casinos to go to, what time of day to gamble, etc.

At one point I remember the therapist asking a woman "How did you feel after a big win?". To the inexperienced therapist it probably seemed like an innocent question, but to the addicted gambler that kind of question turbo-charges the dopamine dump and inspires an immediate desire to go gamble. I asked the woman after the session if she thought the group discussion was helpful for her. She answered that, after the previous week's session, she had gambled six straight days!

The point is that when talking to a therapist you will be directly facing your addiction. And even with an experienced therapist who knows the right questions to ask, your mind may wander off into thoughts that create strong urges to gamble. This can't be avoided. But, as discussed many times before, prepare (while you are thinking clearly) for that possibility. Leave your credit cards and cash at home, or better yet, with your spouse or partner. Tell them not to give them back until the morning. Use the drive home to practice the urge management tools that you will learn in a later chapter in this book. Be aware that this might happen in therapy, or a GA meeting, or any time that you will be confronting your addiction directly. Be aware and be prepared!

Therapy is where you can start to recover. You need to have someone to talk to about the shame, guilt, confusion, depression - all the careening emotions that are a result of your addiction. Do not suffer alone. Make the leap, ask for help. Get a therapist.

Chapter 6

Gamblers Anonymous

"God, give us grace to accept with serenity
the things that cannot be changed,
Courage to change the things
which should be changed,
and the Wisdom to distinguish
the one from the other."

Reinhold Niebuhr

Just a wild guess, but I think everyone in this country has known someone who has attended an Alcoholics Anonymous meeting. Probably they know people who still attend and remain sober. I have a close family member who just got his 44-year pin. He has been attending meetings for 44 years (maybe he missed a dozen meetings during that time) and has *remained sober for 44 years!* As a person fighting addiction, I cannot express how proud (and in awe!) of him I am for his dedication to AA and his continued sobriety. And during that time, because of his experience, he has helped and sponsored many other alcoholics in their quest for sobriety. He is the perfect example of the success of AA and the twelve-step model.

Gamblers Anonymous was founded in 1957 and based directly on the AA model. On their website - www.gamblersanonymous.org - you can find all the information you might want to know about the GA organization, so I won't bore you with it here. I would suggest that you do go to the site and take the 20 question test that will determine if you have a problem with gambling. If you answer yes to 7 of them, they consider you to be a problem gambler (I answered yes to 18 of the 20).

I think I've attended six different GA meetings over the course of my quest to live a gambling-free life. And like finding a therapist (and pretty much everything else) some were good, and some weren't. GA is not anything close to AA in terms of total membership or the number of available meetings. If you live in a heavily populated area you will probably have several choices of places and times. I live in a rural area and, unfortunately, my closest meeting is sixty miles away. The GA website has a location finder, but before you make the drive to the meeting be sure to check to find out if the meeting still exists. The best way to check is to call the location of the meeting.

Also, like finding a therapist, shop around until you find a meeting to your liking. My experience is that GA meetings have a wide range of attendees and quality of the experience. Once again, the nature of us problem gamblers works against this treatment option. The fact that problem gamblers are so secretive and so unwilling to admit or discuss their addiction works against GA having the overall numbers and the same vitality as AA meetings.

I once attended a meeting in a large city for the first time only to see someone there who I knew well and who I never would have suspected had a gambling problem. We were both embarrassed and it was extremely uncomfortable. I never went back, and I'm guessing neither did the other person. I doubt this would have happened at an AA meeting. A good example of our shame and secrecy in action.

This aversion to letting anyone in on our secret gambling life, our secret shame, is the biggest hurdle to overcome in any treatment in order to recover. This quote is from the previously referenced 2016 Survey of Problem Gambling Services in the United States:

"In 2016, about one quarter of one percent of people (14,375) who needed gambling disorder treatment received publicly funded care from a gambling treatment specialist. These figures are revealing when compared to substance use treatment statistics that find 10.8 percent of people aged 12 or older (2.3 million people) who needed substance use treatment received treatment at a specialty facility in 2015. "

That's a 40 to 1 ratio of substance abuse sufferers seeking treatment vs. gamblers seeking treatment. In other words, substance abusers are 40 times more likely then problem gamblers to seek treatment - i.e., to find a therapist, or an inpatient program, or to attend an AA meeting. It's likely that this ratio is also accurate (if not higher) for GA attendance vs. AA attendance.

However, do not let those statistics keep you from considering attending GA meetings. I'll give you two good reasons to go. First, as I emphasized in the chapter on finding a therapist, you need someone to talk to. That very reluctance to share your embarrassment and shame is the exact reason that you need to share. One thing every GA meeting is guaranteed to have is other problem gamblers that you can talk to. You will find, surprisingly, that they are just like you in many ways. You will discover that you are not alone. This is different from your therapist, who likely does not have a gambling problem. The attendees are in different stages of recovery and can offer help and advice for you if you are just starting your recovery. Second, GA, like AA and all of its spin-offs, are based on the 12-step program. While there are some people who have mixed feelings about the 12-step program, there are clearly countless people who feel it has saved them.

If you can find a good meeting, stick with it. If the "God" issue troubles you, find a way to live with it. Keep going until it works for you. Your recovery is more important than finding minor faults with the GA program. Give it a good try.

I think it is appropriate to end this chapter, as all GA meetings do, with the 12-step abbreviated version of the Serenity Prayer.

God grant me the serenity to accept the things I cannot change, the courage to change the things I can, and the wisdom to know the difference.

Chapter 7

Inpatient Programs

"You can keep your drugs
and your whiskey sours.
We got us a higher power!

A chant from the movie *28 Days*
(Watch it if you are thinking about inpatient treatment)

When was the last time you went 30 days without gambling? I'm guessing years, right? A thirty-day inpatient program at a facility dedicated to gambling addiction is worth a try simply for that experience alone. Thirty full days without gambling (and thirty days of not drinking, or drug use) will allow your brain to return to the normal state that nature intended. You will get to know "clear thinking" for the first time in years.

Of course, that is not the only reason to enroll in an inpatient treatment program (otherwise, you could just go to Hawaii for thirty days). In a specific gambling addiction treatment center, you will work with very experienced counselors. You will do exercises, step programs, assessments, one-on-one counseling, and many hours of group therapy. All these activities will allow you to understand your addiction (and yourself) to a degree that you have never considered possible.

Along with the program itself, you will also be with other addicted gamblers who you will form strong bonds with based on your shared addiction, and your shared desire to recover. I am fortunate to be able to attest to the value and beauty of these relationships as I have attended the inpatient treatment at Vanguard/Project Turnabout in Granite Falls Minnesota.

I will say without reservation that it was one of the best experiences of my life. I even liked the daily routine and the food! I'm not going to do an in-depth personal Yelp review here. I'll just say that depending on where you are in your addiction, it can be life-changing.

The expense and the time-off from work (or life) are the big obstacles to this treatment option. The cost is generally in the $10,000 to $25,000 range. If you are in treatment with a state-sponsored therapist, they can work with your state to see if an inpatient program can be funded for you. Many states will pay for this if they think you qualify. There are a lot of variables that are considered by the state in coming to that decision, so I can't offer any advice or assurance that they can or will do this. But, start with this contingency. If it was up to me, an option for inpatient treatment would be funded by the state or federal government for everyone who needed it. Our governments are complicit in gambling addiction. They make millions of dollars by supporting gambling (unlike drugs, for example), so they owe it to you to help you recover from your addiction.

If the state can't pay, try your insurance or your employer. Also, the treatment center itself may offer financing and long-term payment plans. But even if you or your family end up paying, it will be worth it! If an inpatient program can start you on the path to a gambling free life, you know you will earn that $10,000 back quickly, simply by not sticking money in those soul-sucking machines. While the money you will save by not playing slots is important, what value can you put on the bliss of living a life free of gambling?

Gambling addiction inpatient treatment centers come in two flavors: pure and mixed. There are four treatment centers in the United States of the pure variety, i.e. they treat only gambling addiction. There are probably hundreds in the mixed category. Mixed treatment facilities deal primary with substance abuse addictions (alcohol, drugs, etc.), but many also claim to treat gambling addiction.

The four dedicated gambling addiction inpatient treatment centers are:

Algamus Gambling Treatment Services in the Prescott Valley of Arizona
www.algamus.org
Private, 10 beds

Bridgeway Recovery   Santium House   Salem Oregon
https://www.bridgewayrecovery.com/treatment_resid
ential_problem_gambling.php
Private, 8 beds

Core Center of Recovery   Shreveport Louisiana
http://www.helpforgambling.org/core
State supported, 21 beds

Vanguard Center for Gambling Recovery at Project Turnabout   Granite Falls Minnesota
https://www.projectturnabout.org/treatment/gamblin
g-recovery/vanguard
Private, 20 beds

There are many things to consider when choosing an inpatient treatment program. I recommend first going to their website and reading everything they offer. Most of them will post pictures of the facility and the location, which are very helpful. The websites do a good job of leaving out important information, so next you will need to call them. Below I've provided some questions that you might ask (some obvious, some not so obvious).

1) The price (duh).

2) Ask if they can check with your insurance to see if it offers coverage.

3) Ask if the state will pay for it in some way - how that works - and what you must do to make that happen.

4) Do they offer some kind of payment plan, financing, or take credit cards?

5) Do they have any other suggestions as to financing your stay?

6) How many dedicated experienced counselors do they have, and will they be on duty when you will be attending (therapists take vacations too)?

7) Double or single rooms? And if they are not full, can you get a single room?

8) How many other patients are in residence currently, and how many will be in residence when you will be attending?

9) What kind of privileges do you have for leaving the facility (to go on walks for example)?

10) What kind of exercise and leisure activities do they offer?

11) What is the food situation?

12) What do they do to help you after release from treatment?

I'm sure you can come up with many more questions after you have read the information on their website. Just make certain that you inquired about absolutely everything you can think of because once you start, once you show up, you are committed.

Amazing, isn't it? Those are the only "28 day" inpatient treatment options specifically focused on gambling addiction. There are just 59 beds for 5 million problem gamblers. In contrast, over 2 million people received inpatient treatment annually for substance abuse in over 15,000 facilities across the country.

As mentioned above, many of these 15,000 substance abuse centers also claim to have a "gambling addiction track" of some kind. It is entirely possible that these facilities can provide a productive experience for the addicted gambler. They can certainly provide thirty days free of gambling and drinking. And if you are suffering from other serious and treatable conditions (as most of us are), these facilities are equipped and prepared to help with all of your other treatable problems. I would suggest that in addition to the questions I recommended above, you inquire in depth about how they specifically treat gambling addiction when you call them.

The editorial board (me) of the think-tank responsible for writing this book (me again) would now like to make an editorial statement about inpatient treatment. I have attended Vanguard at Project Turnabout in Granite Falls Minnesota for a full term of thirty days. I found it to be exceedingly valuable for addressing my gambling addiction, and it provided many insights that helped me with life in general.

Vanguard is a dedicated gambling treatment program. All patients there are addicted gamblers. I believe this is very important. The staff therapists are gambling addiction trained and experienced. But, as opposed to the three other dedicated facilities, Vanguard is part of a much bigger facility that also treats substance abuse. This allows Vanguard to offer things like a full size gym, weight room, a full time physical fitness instructor, Yoga and craft instructors, an excellent kitchen and salad bar, 24 hour staffing, a large well equipped, well-staffed medical wing, and many other amenities that the other smaller dedicated facilities can't offer.

Vanguard has contracts with several other states. For example, people from Washington State can go there on a state paid scholarship. Vanguard does not try to be an executive or luxurious facility as so many other substance abuse centers aspire to, so they are reasonably priced compared to other options.

There should be twenty more facilities in this country like Vanguard. Maybe someday. End of editorial board editorial.

So, if you can make it work with your schedule and budget, try inpatient. The thirty-day break from gambling (and everything else in your world) will be life altering.

Chapter 8

Smart Recovery and online support groups

"SMART Recovery recognizes the only one who can become truly expert on your recovery is you."
From smartrecovery.org website

I mentioned in the chapter on Gamblers Anonymous that one of the primary benefits of attending a GA meeting was the fellowship of others like you, others who are addicted, others who understand. Unfortunately, there are some people who cannot relate to the specifics of the GA program. The concerns that many people have with GA (and the Anonymous programs in general) can be broken down into three issues:

1) The strong emphasis on a belief in God. The programs claim that the only way to recover from your addiction is to admit you are powerless to help yourself with your addiction, and that you need to turn your recovery over to a "Higher Power". In today's world, they now try to make that concept more acceptable to atheists and agnostics by saying that the higher power can be of your own choosing. I had someone in a meeting once tell me that the higher power could be something as simple as the chair I was sitting on. In other words, I would have to turn over the recovery from my addiction to the chair that I currently had my butt planted in. Come on - there is no way that would work.

Despite these recent confused efforts to be more inclusive of those who are not believers, the program clearly works best for those who have a good and strong belief in God. Of course, there are billions of people in that category, and for those people the higher power part of the program is a strong positive.

2) All of the Anonymous programs emphasize the 12-step program created by Bill Wilson, the founder of AA. The 12-step model has worked for millions of people over many decades. It has saved countless lives, families, and relationships. You must admit it has been successful. However, one of the often-mentioned objections to the 12-step program is how dogmatic it is. This is a bit simplified, but the objection goes like this: If you (the addict) work the program, you will recover, but if you don't recover, it's because you didn't work the program.

Here is a quote from the AA big book:

"Those who do not recover are people who cannot or will not completely give themselves to this simple program, usually men and women who are constitutionally incapable of being honest with themselves...They are naturally incapable of grasping and developing a manner of living which demands rigorous honesty."

In other words, if the 12-steps do not work for you, obviously you are weak and dishonest. We know a lot more about addiction now (and certainly more than Bill Wilson and Bob Smith knew eighty years ago) and calling an addict who has relapsed weak and dishonest is probably not helpful.

3) AA was created in 1935. GA was started in 1957. I think I'm safe in asserting that we know orders of magnitude more about addiction now than we did back in the thirties and fifties. The AA methods, the dogmatic culture, and the written materials (especially true of GA) are stuck in a time before most of today's addicts were even born.

Unfortunately, these Anonymous programs cannot adapt. There are so many meetings, and they are so standardized, that it would take a major overhaul to incorporate even the smallest change. While the Anonymous programs have proven to be one way (and millions would say a good way) to treat addiction, we now have many other options based on our increased experience and our expanded knowledge of addiction.

Smart recovery was started in 1994 as an alternative to the Anonymous programs. Here is the Wikipedia description:

"SMART Recovery is an international non-profit organization that provides assistance to individuals seeking abstinence from addiction. SMART stands for Self-Management and Recovery Training. The SMART approach is secular and science-based, using cognitive behavioral therapy and non-confrontational motivational methods."

Smart recovery is similar to the AA and GA model in that they hold weekly meetings for recovering addicts. These meetings are led by peers and offered at no cost. The difference is that instead of the 12-step process, the content of the meetings is made up of current exercises, tips, techniques, etc. These methods are gathered from many of the recent ideas employed by addiction therapists and treatment facilities.

There are many videos available online that go into depth about these exercises (see the links in the references section for this chapter). I recommend spending a rainy (or snowy) afternoon watching these videos. Not only will you learn about Smart Recovery, you can also do the exercises along with the videos and perhaps learn some things about your addiction.

I did exactly that not long ago. It was a video that explained one of Smart Recovery's main tools called CBA. CBA is simply a cost/benefit analysis of your personal addiction. There are four parts to fill in: The costs to you of living with your addiction, the benefits to you (!) of living in your addiction, the costs to you if you were living an addiction free life, and (of course) the benefits to you if you could live an addiction free life. Sounds simple, right? It turns out that it is surprising insightful.

I recommend that you watch the video on Smart Recovery's CBA exercise and then do it yourself. But, again a warning: Be prepared to combat the urges that might occur as you weigh the costs and benefits of your addiction (the video is identified in the references section of this book).

This may be helpful to you. I'll go through my answers to the Smart Recovery CBA exercise. The CBA works for any addiction, but my answers will be specifically for my gambling addiction. I'll limit my answers to five responses in each section.

Question: What are the *costs* to you for living with your (gambling) addiction?

1) Financial damage (Duh!)
2) Relationships suffer (from isolating, deceiving, shame and guilt)
3) Physical health suffers (the extreme sensory overload, withdrawal, screwed up brain)

4) Self-esteem damage (why can't I stop? I'm weak, I'm a loser)
5) The gambling monkey in brain won't shut up (I'm either trying to stop or planning to go. I can't get it out of my brain.)

Question: What are the *benefits* to you for living with your addiction?

1) A reward to me for accomplishing some goal (motivation to get stuff done)
2) Relieves boredom (especially true for retired seniors)
3) It's what I do, who I am (I'm a gambler, and an expert at slots)
4) Stress relief (When I'm pushing the button there is no room for any other thoughts)
5) The thrill of the big win (I got the bonus! Finally!)

These two questions encapsulate the cost and benefit to you for living with your addiction. Look at them in their entirety. Which list has the most power? Clearly, the costs far outweigh the benefits. But the benefit list can provide insight into why you gamble, and with that it provides opportunities for you to address those reasons in order to stop. In the next chapter (on Cognitive Behavioral Therapy) I'll do just that - I'll take my list and learn a new way to think about each point. Stay tuned.

Question: What will be the *benefits* for you if you could lead an addiction free life?

1) My finances would improve (I could buy things I've been putting off)
2) I could stop isolating myself (See friends, make new relationships)
3) My mental health would improve (Brain chemistry back to normal)
4) Restore my integrity (No more lying and deceit)
5) I would get the gambling monkey out of my brain (free it up for better things)

Question: What will you *hate* about living an addiction free life?

1) Boredom!
2) No more fantasy thinking about big wins
3) No more "I'm a bad-boy gambling-man" personality delusions
4) Will need to find new ways to motivate myself for jobs I don't want to do
5) Recovery is forever, that's a big commitment!

These two questions provide the opportunity for you to imagine what it would be like to live an addiction-free life. I'm guessing that you have never sat yourself down and seriously tried to see, feel, and project what your life would be like if you could eliminate your addiction forever - if you never had to deal with it again - ever!

Try that thought experiment now. Say to yourself "I'm done, I'm free, it's over!!" Put yourself totally into that new life. Go with that thought, play it out. You probably now have a smile emerging! I did this exact thing and it became a magic moment for me and one of the essential lessons of my recovery.

The CBA exercise is one of many tools that Smart Recovery uses, so try to attend a meeting and learn about the rest. To find out about meeting locations and times, go to the Smart Recovery website (www.smartrecovery.org) where they have a meeting finder just like GA.

There is no reason that you cannot attend both GA and Smart Recovery meetings. It's not like going to a Catholic mass early in the morning and a Baptist revival in the afternoon. Do both! They can both help you recover.

Online support groups

I'm not the right person to offer any help about using online groups for problem gambling support. I'm wary of unnamed anonymous people (if they are people) giving me advice over the internet. You don't know if they are old or young, male or female, or if they even have a gambling problem. You can't look them in the eye. But in our new pandemic world, they are often the only option.

If you are unable to attend a meeting due to your location or inability to leave home, perhaps an online support meeting would help you. Both GA and Smart Recovery offer online forums and online meetings (go to their websites for more information).

Because of the pandemic of 2020-2021, online Zoom meetings have become ubiquitous. Several websites are providing dates and times for these GA, AA, Smart Recovery etc. Zoom meetings (two examples: www.recoveryroadonline.com, and www.gamblersinrecovery.com). I'm sure that the GA and Smart Recovery home websites will get into this Zoom directory business in a big way soon.

As the technology improves, and as the participants learn how to structure these meetings, these online meetings have and will become a huge breakthrough for the easy accessibility of help and community.

Other online support options are the many Facebook Groups for addicted gamblers. I belong to a group called "Gamblers Anonymous Support Group". With over ten thousand members it is a vibrant source of information and especially sympathetic support. I recommend joining it to everyone reading this book.

Chapter 9

Cognitive Behavioral Therapy - CBT

"...there is nothing either good or bad, but thinking makes it so."
Hamlet Act 2 Scene 2 - William Shakespeare

"Men are disturbed not by events but by their opinion about events."
Epictetus - Greek Stoic Philosopher 55 AD - 135 AD

At the heart of Cognitive Behavioral Therapy (CBT) is the simple concept that thoughts generate emotions. Often cited as: "Every emotion is preceded by a thought." The specific CBT model is a 4-step process and goes like this: 1) An event occurs, 2) The event causes a thought to arise, 3) The thought creates an emotion, 4) The emotion generates a behavior.

Therefore, if you have a behavior that you want to change, like compulsive gambling, somehow you need to intervene in that 4-step process in order to create a different outcome - i.e. a better behavior.

The only place where you can interrupt that 4-step process is step 2 - your thoughts. We do have some control about what we think after all, especially if you can pause, step back and consider what exactly it was that you just thought. A good CBT therapist will be able to help you manage your thoughts in a more constructive manner. You can learn to have a thought, pause to consider that thought, back up and figure out where that thought came from, and then change that thought to something that generates a more positive outcome. That is what CBT therapists do.

CBT has become the "go to" therapy for addiction these days, and this is specifically true for gambling addiction. While doing the research for gambling addiction inpatient treatment, I noticed that all (also stipulated to be 97.6%) of those mixed facilities (primarily substance abuse treatment centers that claim they have a gambling addiction program as well) say they use CBT. Then they offer some form of this comment about CBT and gambling: "*CBT is especially helpful at correcting the delusional thinking that characterizes compulsive gambling, such as the belief that one can win in spite of repeated, devastating losses.*"

I've read some version of that sentence dozens of times on treatment facility websites. Some go on to elaborate, saying that *if* the addicted gambler can be shown that in the long run they will lose money, they will stop gambling. That if the gambler can change their thoughts from "I will win" to "I will lose", things will get better for them.

Perhaps this is just another instance of whoever it was that created these websites Googled other similar websites and simply copied and pasted those paragraphs. This is an example of Naveen's third law of the internet: "If an untruth is copied and pasted across the internet more than a thousand times, it will become truth". In any case, a facility that makes that claim should be avoided. First of all, that comment is not CBT. It is simply a warning about consequences. It is no different than telling a person if they don't stop smoking, they will likely get lung cancer, or if they don't stop eating so many sweets, they will become diabetic. If you continue to gamble, you will lose money. Duh.

Secondly, that specific substituted thought (that they will lose) is patently not true. All compulsive slot players know that in the long run they will lose. Casinos will even brag about "The best slot return in the state, 93%!" The casinos are so proud of the fact that they will slowly take all your money that they put that info up on the wall in neon lights!

Trust me, addicted slot players understand that over time they will lose. But they also know that this time they might win and win big! They know that is true because it has happened to them many times in the past. We all go to the casino thinking that this time we might just win. Because many (or enough) times we have won.

CBT *can* work for addicted gamblers. Let me give you a specific example that actually makes sense. Consider this story: You have a good friend who you haven't seen for too long, and tonight the two of you have planned to have dinner at a favorite restaurant. You planned this weeks ago and have been really looking forward to it. Then you get a call from your friend the afternoon of the dinner and she says that she's sorry but cannot make the dinner. The conversation is abrupt, the excuse a bit squishy, and she seems a little off. This is the event part of the 4 step CBT concept.

The thoughts (step 2) that occur to you right after ending the call go like this: She blew me off. She obviously did not want to see me. I thought we were friends. How disrespectful! I wonder what I did. These thoughts immediately set off emotions (step 3) of anger, disappointment, and sadness (I'm not liked). So, now you are feeling this mish-mashed-assortment of very negative emotions. And, well golly gee, guess what, now you also have a free evening and the cash in your pocket that you were going to spend on dinner and drinks. I wonder what an addicted gambler would do in this circumstance? Hmm, I'm guessing that nearly all of the time it will result in a trip to the casino.

In this little story, all the CBT steps are present: event, thoughts, emotions, and behavior. To change that negative behavior (going to the casino), CBT asks you to go back and examine your thoughts. Why did you think those things? What other thoughts could you have had that wouldn't have resulted in going to the casino?

Well, you could have thought that maybe something was wrong with her, or maybe something happened that made her depressed. Maybe it wasn't you. Maybe she is suffering for some reason. If you had those thoughts instead, you then would have felt worried and empathetic (new and different emotions) and possibly would have called her back (a different behavior!) and said "I'll go get a pizza for us, and stop by your place and we can talk".

Two very different outcomes from the same event are possible by stepping back and making a rational assessment of your thoughts. Seems simple, right? Not exactly. Thinking about your thoughts is not that easy. They are your thoughts after all, so how can you think they are not?

At this point I'll add a wrinkle to the CBT concept. Perhaps those original negative thoughts in the story are *not really* your thoughts? I would offer that in that moment right after the phone call, those thoughts were actually generated by your addiction! Your addiction knew very well that if it could get you to experience negative emotions (feeling bad about yourself) that you would go to the casino. Your addiction (you) knew that this unexpected event was now an opportunity to gamble, and so it produced those ugly thoughts.

I wonder...if you did not have an addiction (of any kind) how would you have dealt with that phone call? Maybe your better angels would have sounded the empathy alarm. I think you would have been worried about your friend and wanted to help her. I think you would have made that call - *if it were not for your addiction*!

When we addicts finally reach the point where we know we have a problem, and when we know we want to stop, from that point on we need to come up with a strong and reasonable excuse of some kind to go use, or go gamble. We become masters at generating these seemingly legitimate excuses for our addictive behavior. This is perhaps the most critical skill that our addiction employs - creative excuse making.

Your addiction always sits idling in your brain, waiting for an opening. In the phone call example above, the first thing that actually occurred after ending that call was the realization (by your addiction) that there was suddenly an opportunity to go gamble - "Wow, she cancelled, now I can justify an excuse to go to the casino!"

But in a way, this may make the substitution of positive thoughts easier. You can blame the faulty thinking on your addiction. You can say to yourself "Hey, that's not me, that's my addiction talking. Screw you addiction, I'm better than that!" And then substitute your better self's more positive thoughts.

For the compulsive gambler, the negative thoughts that your addiction is trying to foist on you are almost always in the form of creating an excuse to justify gambling. So perhaps there is another step in the CBT four-step process that we can identify and consider. Your addiction knows that if it can create the emotions it needs, then you will use those emotions to create a strong excuse and urge to go gamble. And then, of course, you will get in the car and drive to the casino.

In my experience, once in the car, the ballgame's over. I've never turned back. I've thought about it, I've tried, but I've always driven on. Therefore, the place to interrupt the negative CBT process must come before the excuse is decided upon. Go back to the fundamental concept in CBT, which states that the place to interrupt the cycle is in changing your thoughts.

Changing your thoughts is easier *once you have decided to do so*. The really hard part is getting to the point where you are willing to examine your thoughts with the goal of altering them. How can you get to that point? It won't happen immediately after having the negative thoughts appear (following an event). I don't think very many people are prepared to do that - after all, these negative thoughts were still your thoughts.

Perhaps the additional step that I proposed might be the answer. The thing that happens between the negative emotions, and getting in the car, is your "excuse making" step. You need to make an excuse to justify going to the casino when you know that you shouldn't. The excuse making is not an uncontrollable emotional response. It is instead a rational construction based on how you want to deal with the negative emotions.

What if you use that bit of rational thinking as a *trigger* to get you to go back and alter your original thoughts that caused the negative emotions? *What if you could train yourself to recognize your excuse-making, and then train yourself to see that this excuse-making can become the trigger, the time and place for you to stop, back up, and see if your real self can create better thoughts than your addicted self just did?*

Do this: Right now, while you are thinking clearly and can prepare positively (sound familiar?), make a list of all the excuses that you use to justify your gambling. You know them all too well. Keep the list handy, memorize it. *Tell yourself that when your addiction is cramming any one of those excuses into your brain, that this is the trigger to get you to pause, go back, and figure out why this is happening.* What were the emotions? What were the thoughts that caused the emotions? What thoughts would your better-self have had instead?

If you do that, it will deflate that excuse. You will beat your addiction - at least this one time. You can then taunt your addiction, mock it, verbally abuse it. Tell it to go back into its stinky hole and throw dirt on it. And then, if you get into the car, go to Costco instead, where you can put your hard-earned money into half-gallon bottles of mayo and New York strip steaks.

So, go get a therapist who knows CBT. It will help. Fortunately, most therapists do know, and do practice CBT.

Chapter 10

Mindfulness

*"If you want to conquer the anxiety of life, live in the
moment, live in the breath"*
Amit Ray

*"Just as a snake sheds its skin, we must shed our past over
and over again"*
Buddha

Mindfulness has become one of those concepts that we
are exposed to constantly. It seems to be the cure for
almost everything, and maybe it is. Though if I asked
you to describe Mindfulness in only one paragraph,
could you? Probably not. We will let a few others do
that for us:

*The practice of maintaining a nonjudgmental state of
heightened or complete awareness of one's thoughts,
emotions, or experiences on a moment-to-moment basis*

Merriam-Webster Dictionary

Mindfulness is the basic human ability to be fully present, aware of where we are and what we're doing, and not overly reactive or overwhelmed by what's going on around us.

Mindful.org

Mindfulness means to pay attention on purpose, in the present moment, and nonjudgmentally. The emphasis on being "purposeful" is crucial as a counterbalance to the automatic pilot default that inhabits our mind most of the time. You can purposefully bring your attention to your child's smile, to the feeling of the steering wheel, or to the exhale of your breathing. This is mindfulness.

Psychology Today

If your brain is anything like mine (for your sake, I hope it is not) it never shuts up. It is a cascade of thoughts, one after another, some tied together, some random. You are driving along, doing nothing in particular, and you see a car just like the one your ex had. You then remember buying that car, how much it cost, the argument you had about it being too much money, the money you gave up in the divorce, the unfairness of that whole episode, and who knows where else down the rabbit hole it will take you.

Our minds wander into the past and into the future, replaying old mistakes, generating new worries. The resulting emotions range from regret, shame, guilt (the past) to anxiety, fear, and uncertainty (the future). So...here is my uneducated definition of Mindfulness:

It is a learned technique that will get your brain to shut up for a minute or two so you can pause and then hopefully entertain better thoughts. Mindfulness, as expressed in the previous definitions, helps you to become aware of yourself and your surroundings, and it strives to return you to the present. Mindfulness is a purposeful awareness of the present. I think it is fair to say that the more time you spend in the present (as opposed to the past or the future) the happier you will be.

Like many of the ideas and techniques discussed in these chapters on how to quit gambling, mindfulness is also a practice that will help you in your life in general. The problem gambling treatment community often states that 60% to 70% of problem gamblers also suffer from other disorders such as depression or substance abuse.

All the treatments examined in this book can be used to help with these varied disorders, and to improve your general mental wellbeing. Getting a therapist, inpatient treatment, going to AA and GA meetings, CBT, and mindfulness, as well as those treatment options in future chapters, can help you deal with whatever is going on in your life that you would like to change for the better.

Mindfulness even helps healthy people (there may still be some out there). It is a valuable lifetime practice, it's free, it's simple, it's easy to learn, it doesn't require sweating or heavy breathing or getting down on the floor. Anyone can do it anytime and anywhere. There are a gazillion videos, articles, and books available to help you learn how to be mindful.

There is also an eight-week (2-3 hours, one night a week) class called Mindfulness Based Stress Reduction, or MBSR that is available in many places. MBSR has been around for decades and was started by Jon Kabat-Zinn, one of the pioneers in the modern definition of mindfulness. Classes in MBSR are held in most places and are available on-line as well.

If mindfulness can improve your overall wellbeing and happiness, it will certainly help you in dealing with your addiction. There are also several specific places where it can directly be used to help you with trying to change your gambling behaviour. In chapter 2, I mentioned the technique of looking at your hands to snap you back into the present (after walking out of the casino in total despair). This idea seems kind of silly, trivial even, but believe me it can be very impactful. I use it several times a day when my thoughts wander off into the past or the future in a negative way. I can't tell you why it works, but it does.

When we get to the chapter on urge warfare, mindfulness will also play a prominent role in learning how to derail your urge to go to the casino. But I want to address something here specifically about the intersection of mindfulness and slot machine addiction. Remember that mindfulness is a practice that helps you be in the present, that helps you shut off the guilt and shame of the past and shut out the thoughts of fear and anxiety about the future. Mindfulness asks us to live in the present because the present is the only thing we can control.

Guess what? Compulsive slot machine playing, i.e., sitting on that ugly stool, pushing that stupid button for eight hours without a break, does the same thing as mindfulness! Mindfulness asks us to be acutely aware of our current surroundings, of the sights and sounds right in front of us. I can think of no activity, including mindful meditation, that has us slot machine addicts focused so intently on the sights and sounds in the present moment as when we compulsively play a slot machine. And while most people can meditate for several minutes (some even up to an hour or more), us slot machine addicts can push that button for many hours without a break, all the while very mindfully aware of the present sights and sounds.

This is why the treatment professionals call slot machine addiction "escape gambling". This is why those evil machines have such a hold on us. When we sit down on that stool pushing that button, we know we will enter another world, a world outside of our day-to-day existence, outside of that day-to-day world that is too often full of confusing and painful thoughts. In the slot machine world, our focus becomes completely involved with the machine - the visuals, the sounds, the anticipation of a win. There is no room *what-so-ever* for any other thought to intrude into our consciousness. We are totally in the present (for however long it takes to lose all our money). Mindfulness by machine addiction.

Perhaps, if you can recognize that you play those evil machines in order to escape from your negative thoughts, then you can start to figure out a path forward where you don't need to escape. Substitute mindful meditation for slot machine play. Or use CBT to have better ways of thinking about your past and future. Or get a good therapist to help you. I think that this is the Holy Grail of slot machine addiction treatment: If you can eliminate the need for escaping from your negative thoughts, you can eliminate the need to gamble. Make that your quest.

Make the effort, take the time to learn mindfulness and how to work it into your life. You will be a happier, more accepting and content person. For right now, try this: Look at your hands for 10 seconds. Do da do da do do…time's up. Did it work?

Chapter 11

DBT and Self Compassion

*"Be willing to have it so. Acceptance of what has happened is
the first step to overcoming the consequences of any
misfortune."*
William James

*"...forgive us our trespasses as we forgive those who trespass
against us"*
God

Dialectical Behavior Therapy was developed by Dr.
Marsha Linehan in the early 1990's at the University of
Washington. She had been treating patients who had
very difficult psychological problems and who also had
strong suicidal inclinations, but she was having
difficulty making progress. The initial strong resistance
of her patients to treatment was preventing her from
even getting started, so she began putting together a
program to overcome that initial resistance, and DBT
was born.

Dialectical is a tough word. Even looking it up in the dictionary doesn't help. It is a word used to describe a concept that has evolved over the centuries. Of Greek origin, the word simply meant using reason and logic to discuss a problem. Centuries later, it was usurped by philosophers such as Kant, Hegel, and Karl Marx. You may recognize Hegel's Dialectic of "Thesis, Antithesis, Synthesis". If I may be so bold as to summarize Hegel's Dialectic - it means using reasoned and logical dialogue to discuss conflicting viewpoints of a problem in order to come to a satisfactory result (kind of like what our politicians *should* be doing).

Dr. Linehan has further usurped it and applied it to her psychological treatment methodology, DBT. Like CBT, DBT is a behavioral therapy. The goal is to change behaviors that are hurting you. The focus is on the future, not on how your father was being strict with you when you were 10, or on understanding how your dreams relate to your poor eating habits. In behavioral therapy, future "change" is the key concept. I want to stop drinking, I need to quit gambling, I want to not be depressed.

The difficulty Dr.Linehan was having initially with her patients centered on their reluctance, aversion, even revulsion to dealing with their painful past behavior. For example: The 12-step program instructs you to examine your past behavior in depth. It tells you to admit to yourself and others that you are an addict with no hope of changing without the help of a higher power. It asks to identify who you have hurt and make amends to them. The focus is on getting you to confront, even relive, the awful things you have done in the past in order for you to clearly see all of the damage you have done to yourself and others.

Of course (and once again) the 12-step programs have been successful for decades for very many people. But I also think that many other people who start those programs soon quit when they are asked to confront their history in such a painful, in-depth manner.

For the people that Dr. Linehan was trying to help, for those people who were in grave danger but were not able to focus directly on their difficult past, she created a different approach. It was an approach influenced by her deep understanding of Buddhism and Mindfulness. Her approach was to accept that the past cannot be changed, to understand that the past simply "Is what it is".

The idea was to relieve the patient of their constant awareness of the pain and suffering inflicted by the things they had done so they could be free to focus on changing their future behavior. The "acceptance" that she was proposing did not mean that they should accept *that their past behavior was okay*. It wasn't. It means that they accept that they did it, accept that they can't change it, and accept that it does not help them to get better if they continue to suffer from it. To recover, they needed to move on with a healthier and more positive attitude and focus on their hopes for the future.

Like everything discussed in this book, that concept is easier said than done. There are now a whole bunch of terms and ideas surrounding Dr. Linehan's acceptance concept, terms like: Radical Acceptance, Self-Compassion, and Self Forgiveness. Fortunately for you, there are a boatload of good videos on YouTube that can help you get a good grasp of the what and the how of her view of acceptance (go to YouTube and search on Dr. Marsha Linehan).

Now, back to the meaning of Dialectical in DBT. The two competing concepts in DBT are acceptance and change. You accept what you have done, and you also want to change it. The synthesis takes place because it turns out that it is easier to change if you can first move on from your past. Of course, DBT is considerably more comprehensive and complex than my brief statement explaining the dialectical part. You will need to find a trained DBT therapist if you want to understand and pursue the complete treatment.

Let me describe how I believe the concepts in DBT therapy are specifically useful in helping the addicted gambler. Addicted gamblers carry a substantial burden of shame and guilt. Unlike most other addictions and disorders, gambling most often is done in secret. And in order to keep their addiction secret, gamblers will lie, deceive, and steal. Not only are they ashamed about gambling and losing money, they are even more shameful about all the lies and deceptions that they constantly need to employ with their family and friends.

Even before an addicted gambler admits to themselves that they have a problem and that they want to stop, they feel guilt and shame about these lies and deceptions they use to go gamble. They like gambling and they may not want to quit, but they don't like what they do in order to keep it secret. Then, once they decide that they want to quit, another even deeper and more destructive shame appears. *They don't understand why they can't stop!*

Remember that it wasn't until 2013 that the therapeutic community recognized disordered gambling as an actual addiction. In the freshly-out-of-denial mind of the addicted gambler now seeking to stop, and (as they assume) in the minds of their family and friends, the commonly held belief is that if you need to quit gambling - just *stop gambling* - don't go to the casino. How hard can that be! At this early stage of their recovery they likely do not know how their addiction works.

I would assert, and I know this personally from years of living with it, that the shame of not being able to quit, of being too weak to stop, of being unable to do the right thing, unable to do the thing that everyone else that I know could easily do - that weakness, that level of shame changes your life. You can deal with the financial losses, and you can even deal with the lies (they have a short half-life, either you get away with it, or you apologize and say you won't do it again). But the shame, guilt, and loss of respect *for yourself* when you can't make yourself stop, that awful sinkhole of personal failure, never goes away.

Hopefully, at some point in the recovery process, the addicted gambler will learn that they have an addiction, that their brain has been compromised by their gambling behavior, and that it is now preventing them from stopping that behavior. That knowledge will help a little to reduce the shame. The problem that still exists is that your friends and family likely don't know you have an addiction, or they don't really understand what that means. You know that they are judging you, you still feel the helplessness of that judgment, and yet you still don't really understand why you can't stop.

It gets even worse. In order to justify your new reality that you can't quit, that you have an addiction, the thing that will irrefutably prove your inability to quit, and that will show to others that you do, in fact, have an addiction, *is to continue to gamble.* You can then say with confidence to your therapist or family, I have an addiction! I went to the casino again, I can't stop.

Because if I do simply stop, I wouldn't have this inability to stop. My addiction excuse would disappear, and I would have to go back to knowing that I'm stupid and weak and immoral for all the gambling I have done. So, in order to not feel weak, stupid and immoral, I'll run with that addiction idea *and just keep on gambling!*

This is where Dr. Linehan's concept of Radical Acceptance can be very powerful for addicted gamblers. It is a way out of the negative spiral described in the previous paragraphs. Don't get stuck in the guilt and shame cycle. Accept that those things are in your past, cannot be changed, and need to be understood simply as what you've done, not who you are. Then you can move on to finding solutions for your goal of changing future behavior, for your goal of living a gambling free life.

Once you understand the radical acceptance concept of DBT and actually do it, the next step is to get help to actually change your future behavior. DBT provides many tools to help you modify your behavior for the better. Similar to Smart Recovery, DBT has developed practical exercises that can help you understand why and how you need to change. DBT also incorporates Mindfulness extensively in their behavior changing treatment. DBT describes things like everyday acceptance, willingness, distress tolerance, urge surfing, and grounding yourself. These things are all Mindfulness based concepts and can be beneficial in dealing with your gambling addiction and with your life and happiness in general.

The therapeutic professional literature has only a few articles discussing DBT for gambling addiction, and for those that do offer it, more research needs to be done. I'm convinced that DBT can be an extremely successful treatment for gambling addiction, but unfortunately it seems that it has not yet been adopted by professionals or treatment facilities.

With one exception: Free By The Sea is a drug and alcohol treatment facility on the southern Washington coast that focuses on DBT for substance abuse addiction. They also have a specific gambling addiction treatment track using DBT. To my knowledge this is the only program for gambling addiction utilizing DBT. Something to consider.

Self Compassion

Self compassion is perhaps a step beyond radical acceptance. It is an additional way to help drain the pus from the shame/guilt/self-loathing boil of our gambling addiction. Still, and again, it is important to understand that neither radical acceptance nor self-compassion justifies your gambling behavior in the past or in the future. Do not confuse acceptance (or forgiveness) with "acceptable". What we have done - the gambling, lies, deceptions, etc. - is *not* acceptable. Radical acceptance simply means that yes, you did all those things. You gambled and lied and deceived - all of that happened, and you now accept your prior behavior as fact.

Beyond acceptance comes forgiveness. It often happens that the people in our lives do something, or say something, that they should not have said or done. Often these words or actions hurt us. Yet at the time (or in time) we forgive them. Most of us are compassionate people. We are often compassionate to others, but seldom with ourselves. Do you think it might be time, as you work toward your recovery, to forgive yourself? What would that mean to you? Could that possibly free you up and give you strength to focus on your future in a more positive fashion?

There is an excellent website out there that is all about self-compassion. Dr. Kristen Neff has written books, guides for professional therapists, and research papers on self-compassion, and her website (www.self-compassion.org) has good information that can help you learn to forgive. Of interest is her emphasis on mindfulness (that seems to integrate with most every therapy these days). Mindfulness self compassion - what a rich and potent concept.

I will now officially forgive you. You can forgive you too. Time to move on with a hopeful future. You are worth it.

Chapter 12

Willpower

"I can resist everything except temptation"
Oscar Wilde

Why can't I take better care of myself? Why can't I eat better, exercise more, drink less, sleep more (or less)? Why can't I stop gambling? Why can't I do all the things that I know I should do? It's not for the lack of knowledge. I am aware of the proper diet, the right amount of alcohol to drink, the kind of exercise I need to do, and that I shouldn't gamble. It's not for lack of money. All these things that I should be doing will probably save me money. It's not for lack of ability, or health. I know that if I do these things, I'll have more energy and feel better, not worse. So, dammit, please tell me why I don't do the right things for myself!

Probably the first reason that comes to mind is that I lack willpower. I don't have the strength of will to eat better, drink less, stop gambling. I do know other people (but not many) who *can* do all those things. I know a married couple that actually do accomplish all of those things. They are in their seventies and still run marathons. They seem happy, contented and mostly anxiety free (I'm guessing you are expecting me to add right now something like "and don't you just hate them?" But I'm not going to do that.)

What is that couple's secret? Do they simply have more willpower than I do? If so, where did they get that extra willpower? Did they read a book that told them where to find more willpower? Did they see a therapist who told them how to strengthen their willpower? Was there a class? Or were they just born with more willpower than the rest of us? Am I simply willpower deficient? I must be. I can't think of another explanation.

But what exactly is willpower and where does it come from? Willpower, or self-control, is the ability to resist immediate temptations in order to achieve long-term goals. "I'm having a bad day, I want to eat two Whoppers, have a cigarette, break out the ice cream, and go gamble". As opposed to, "I'm having a bad day, I want to go for a walk, call my Mom, work on my book". Clearly, the strength of our willpower is not fixed. It varies by the circumstances, the time of day, and guess what? It is, once again, based on those darn brain chemicals!

Everything that you might want to learn about willpower can be found in an excellent recent book by Roy Baumeister and John Tierney called (not surprisingly) *Willpower*. I will be using their ideas extensively in this chapter, as it turns out (again, not surprisingly) that there is not a lot of written material about willpower, especially in relation to gambling addiction.

The concept of willpower is considered to be a problem, not a solution, by many professionals in the addiction recovery business. The 12-step programs are in some respects based on the failure of a person's willpower to keep them from drinking alcohol, or taking drugs, or gambling. These quotes are from the AA Big Book:

"The fact is that most alcoholics, for reasons yet obscure, have lost the power of choice in drink. Our so-called will power becomes practically nonexistent."

"Our whole trouble had been the misuse of will power. We had tried to bombard our problem with it instead of attempting to bring it into agreement with God's intention for us.

Step 3: *"Made a decision to turn our will and our lives over to the care of God as we understood Him."*

In the 12-step program, the reason you are successful in recovery is because you stopped trying to impose your willpower on your addiction and have instead turned your recovery over to a higher power.

But if our personal willpower is unable to conquer our addiction, then how do you explain all the people who are in long-term recovery who don't believe in a higher power? How did they recover? Fortunately, there are many paths to dealing with addiction that don't involve a higher power.

The many not God-based ideas, techniques, processes, and trained helpers can all assist you in dealing with your addiction. But guess what, in the end it is *always* your willpower that keeps you in recovery! How can it be anything else? We all have free will (assume that's true for now). Therefore, your ability to decide to not gamble is, in that moment of decision, your own willpower making it so.

Initially, your lack of willpower may have been a part of the problem, but in the end, it is also the solution. Heresy! Fool! I can hear all the twelve-steppers, and many of the therapists now going "Boo, Hiss". Once again, they are saying, "Mr. Dahl, you have clearly proven that you are not a professional in this addiction business (yes, that is a true thing, I am nothing close to a professional, please keep that in mind)".

If I am willpower deficient, and currently cannot stop doing the things I know I shouldn't be doing, is there any way to possibly strengthen my willpower in order to help me do the right things? Yes, there is! According to Baumeister and Tierney there are some fairly easy things you can do. How about having a big glass of orange juice in the afternoon? Huh, really, explain please (you say). Okay, I will.

(An aside: I have read many books in the course of doing research for this book. Two stand out, and I highly recommend that everyone in the treatment profession read them - the Baumeister book I'm discussing here, and Jessie Bering's book *Suicidal*.)

Tierney and Baumeister's book details many fascinating studies undertaken over the years to try to understand how some people are better at resisting temptation. The very short version goes like this: Self-regulation (willpower) is a function of brain chemistry. The brain requires glucose as fuel to keep willpower effective. As the glucose available to the brain is depleted, the strength of a person's willpower declines. Baumeister named this process of reduced glucose causing reduced willpower "Ego Depletion".

His book describes many of the hundreds of tests undertaken that prove his conclusion. It is worth reading just for the descriptions and fascinating results of these experiments. It appears to me that Baumeister's conclusion regarding glucose and willpower is indisputable.

I'll describe these experiments in general terms. They begin with a large group of people doing some activity that requires focused willpower. For example, they ask the group to watch a laugh-out-loud comedy, but require them to never laugh or smile for the whole duration of the movie. This requires two hours of constant use of their willpower. Next, they give half the group a large glass of sugared juice, and the other half a sugar-free drink. Then they ask the group to work on a complex geometry problem for as long as they can to solve it (however, they don't know that the problem is unsolvable). The results were that the group that got the non-sugar drink could only work for eight minutes before giving up, but the group that got the sugar drink could work for over twenty minutes.

This general format of the experiment has been performed many times and is believed to conclusively prove Baumeister's concept of "Ego Depletion" - i.e., during the exercise of willpower the brain consumes glucose. It turns out that you can increase the strength of your willpower by drinking a large glass of orange juice to replenish your glucose!

Baumeister and Tierney cite several frightening examples of ego depletion effects in real life. An Israeli study of parole board hearings showed that an inmate would be six times more likely to have their parole approved if they appeared before the parole board in the morning as opposed to the afternoon. The parole board members had to concentrate on each case and, as the day wore on, their ability to focus withered, which led them to choose the easy way out and deny parole. The same statistical patterns show up for appearing before a judge for a crime. People who appeared in the morning were five times more likely to get a light sentence as those who appeared in the afternoon.

The book goes on to propose several things that can increase your willpower based on the ego depletion concept. For example, any use of your willpower will deplete the glucose needed for another use of willpower. For that reason, you should only work on one personal issue at a time. Therefore, don't try to lose weight, or quit smoking, while in the early stages of recovery from your gambling addiction.

It's possible that anyone fighting any addiction has an underlying blood sugar problem. Many people walk around these days with undiagnosed diabetes or hypoglycemia (chronic low blood sugar). Lethargy, depression, and poor decision making are common to addictive behaviors, and they are the same symptoms you might have with blood sugar diseases.

Check for those diseases if you are fighting an addiction. See your doctor for blood tests. You can even go online and get a blood sugar level test kit that contains everything you need to test your levels several times a day for a month. I did exactly that a while back when I thought I might have diabetes. The kit costs 25 to 50 bucks and the procedure is simple.

If nothing else, keep a bottle of orange juice around and when you are dragging, don't go to the casino, just have a big glass. Replenish your ego.

Chapter 13

Urge Warfare

"Whenever the devil harasses you, seek the company of men or drink more, or joke and talk nonsense, or do some other merry thing."
Martin Luther

"Better to shun the bait, than struggle in the snare."
John Dryden

Your mission, if you chose to accept it, is to *understand, fight, and ultimately defeat* your urge to go gamble. Here's a bold statement: If you can win these battles, you will stop gambling. What would happen if every time you got that strong urge to go gamble you fought it, wrestled it to the ground, stomped on its throat till it croaked, and then kicked it into the gutter? Seriously, how fun would that be? How good would that feel?

You know how it happens. You are driving back from a dentist appointment and your addiction slips into your head and says: "Hey, the casino is only a half-hour away from here, and it would be a good place to let that Novocain wear off. Just turn left up here at the overpass". And then, without even considering your prior commitments to yourself, or your promises to others, you make the turn, and there you go again...

The urges hit us, it seems, when we are least prepared. They make their siren arguments seem so logical and acceptable. You must admit, our addiction is really good at this. This is why (again) we must prepare as best we can, ahead of time, when we are sensible and strong. There are many things we can do when confronted with an overwhelming urge to gamble. You have already learned several powerful techniques by reading this book.

Use your CBT skills to back up and find the origin of the urge. Use your mindfulness skills to bring yourself simply into the present (where your urge has no power). Call your GA sponsor.

In this chapter I'll add several more ideas that you can employ both ahead of time, and at the moment of decision (to not turn left at the off-ramp). But first you must understand that battling urges is in fact warfare - mortal combat, a sometimes-literal life-and-death struggle. Think of the 10,000 suicide victims last year who might still be alive today if they had won that battle with their urge on their fateful day. Believe this: This next urge might be *your* life-or-death battle. You need to win it. Prepare. Arm yourself. Fight as if your life depended on it. Because it does. What follows are your weapons in this fight.

Directed Imagery

Separate yourself (the real you) from your addiction. Give your addiction (and the voice it uses to urge you to gamble) a name and a picture. I call mine Kenny, after Kenny Rodgers the Gambler, though the image I create for Kenny is not nearly that handsome. I visualize Kenny as looking like Gollum from Lord of The Rings - a hairless, slimy, smelly, little, ugly, dishonest creature. Kenny lives in a hole in the ground, and only pops up to tempt and to convince me to go gamble. When he does emerge, I grab an eight-foot fence post, and then pound him in the head, butt end first, until he is a bloody gooey mess in the bottom of his hole. Screw you Kenny.

Well, yes, it is excessively violent. But I have spoken directly to Baba Rom Com, one of the gurus, one of the masters of non-violence, and he has assured me that in the use of directed imagery, violence and profanity are not only acceptable, they are required.

You can of course pick your own name and visual for your addiction. The important part is to separate yourself from your addiction so that you can clearly define your opponent. Do that now. Take a few minutes to come up with your addiction's name, then decide on your own version of its violent and horrifying defeat. It's a fun thing to practice while driving home from work or Starbucks.

Urge Surfing - Accept, Separate, and Wait

Urges are a normal part of your recovery. They will always be with you in one form or another. Just as what we are instructed to do during mindful meditation, when we have thoughts, and we accept them just as thoughts, and then we let them pass, simply accept the urge as an urge and as something that is normal during your recovery, and then mindfully allow it to slip away. Urges have a very short half-life - they will lose their power over you in less than a half-hour. Know that it will pass if you can just wait a while.

I watched a good TEDx talk video titled "The Secret to Self Control" by Jonathan Bricker (see the references section at the end of this book). He discusses a specific urge surfing idea that he calls "Willingness". Though it is very much the same as the general mindfulness urge surfing of DBT and other proponents of mindfulness, his demo of how to do it provides a good picture of a powerful mindfulness idea. It goes like this: You experience an urge (as I have been all week while writing this chapter), then you step back, both metaphorically and literally, and say to yourself "I'm having an urge that makes me want to go gamble". Then you pause. Then you again step away a few more paces and say to yourself "Now I'm noticing that I'm having a thought that creates an urge and makes me want to go gamble".

Bricker stops at that point and explains that the additional qualifiers "I'm having a thought, and I'm noticing I'm having a thought", along with the physical and symbolic stepping away, create an actual separation between you and the craving. This separation weakens the craving and makes it seem to be outside you, and *not inside* you, and the craving loses its much of its power over you.

I would add an additional step, both literally and figuratively, to Bricker's process. I suggest that you again pause and step away a few more paces, and then say to yourself "Now I notice that the craving is going away". Then look at your hands to snap you back to the present, thereby symbolically closing out the craving episode, and then get back to whatever business you were doing before the craving appeared. And, as you walk away with a smile on your face, say "That was cool!"

Bricker promotes an important recovery tool - separation. The more you can separate yourself from your addiction, the better you will be able to apply the many ideas in this book. CBT, mindfulness, DBT, acceptance, self-compassion. All these techniques require a degree of separation between you and your addiction. Work on that separation. It is important.

Use the urge as a positive trigger

Turn the tables on the urge. When it pops up, use it to do something positive. Have the urge itself be a trigger for *good* behavior. Plan ahead so that you can act on that trigger. Promise yourself you will go clean the bathroom when the urge tries to lure you to the casino. Go rake the yard. Go for a long walk. Go visit your aunt in the assisted-living home.

By doing this you won't reward the urge, instead you will use it to accomplish something that will make you feel good (and maybe get the same dopamine rush you would have gotten at the casino). Make the urge your bitch.

Use your CBT skills

The urge you are experiencing came from somewhere. In the chapter on Cognitive Behavioral Therapy, the four stages of a behavior were discussed - an event happens, it causes a thought to occur, the thought creates an emotion, and the emotion leads to a behavior. Often the urge you are experiencing is a result of exactly this process. Something happens and the next thing you know you are in the car headed to the casino.

When the urge hits you, use what you learned about CBT. What was the event? What was the thought? What was the subsequent emotion that created the excuse to go gamble? Back up your awareness to the point at which the urge started. Then go back to the event and try to find a better thought than the one you had.

In the CBT chapter I also discussed how our addiction is good at making excuses. So, think now about the excuse you are using this time to justify your trip to visit those evil machines. This is a good place to do battle. Attack that excuse. Give it a name and a face just like the directed imagery above. You are better than this lame excuse. It is invalid. It has no power over you. You are stronger than it.

Lots of other ideas - do your research

Urge management, urge control, urge surfing, self-control - these are all terms used to describe that critical moment when you must decide if you want to go with your addiction, or stay in your recovery. Use these terms above to search the internet for all sorts of methods to beat your urges. You will find a year's worth of reading and videos to watch. All the addiction treatments centers need to put a strong emphasis on dealing with urges, and so they do.

Justifying going to war

I have named this chapter "Urge Warfare" for a reason. What is recovery? Recovery is simply winning the battle of your recovered self, vs. that damn addiction. And for us addicted gamblers that battle is *too often* a life or death fork in our journey.

Think once again about the 10,000 or more addicted gamblers that every year walk out of the casino, and within hours kill themselves! One day they were living their life, then they experienced an urge, and then they lost their battle with the urge. Now they are dead. Had they won that battle; they would still be alive.

The treatment community is fond of issuing broad generalizations about addiction and then repeating them down the line, as gospel. One such generalization currently in vogue is that you should not fight your urge, as that will only make it stronger. First of all, that idea is patently not true. The alternative to fighting it is giving in to it - not a good plan. Of course, if by fighting the urge they mean sitting down, clenching your fists until your knuckles are white, and saying "I'm not going to do it" over and over again, then maybe they are right. Obviously, that method of fighting will not work.

The white-knuckling and simply-saying-no version of fighting urges is like bringing a feather to a knife fight. The fighting that I'm recommending is based on arming yourself with big weapons: CBT, Imagery, Separation, Mindful Urge Surfing, etc. These are powerful weapons that you can use effectively to overwhelm your urge. Now, by using what you have learned, you are bringing an assault rifle to the knife fight. All you need to do is use your weapons...and be *resolved* to win.

Of course, this does not mean that you should *not* do the essential recommendation of this book - preparing for a relapse. The very specific process described in chapter 2 (*Please Don't Kill Yourself Today*) will save your life.

Keep fighting those urges But if you do happen to lose, make sure you have prepared for that relapse. Just stay alive, and then *live* to fight and win again.

Chapter 14

Financial Controls

*"Money, like emotions, is something you must control to
keep your life on the right track."*
Natasha Munson

Starve the beast

Luckily for us, there is still one feature of a slot
machine that we can use to our advantage - the
machines only work when you slip actual cash money
into the slot. They don't (yet) directly take credit cards.
God help us if that changes.

If you don't have bills in your pocket, you can't gamble. Doesn't matter if you want to, doesn't matter if you are in the casino with a drink in your hand, it doesn't matter what your state of mind is - if you don't have cash, you won't be able to gamble. I'm stating and repeating the obvious here because eliminating your ability to acquire cash is a foolproof way to stop gambling without having to rely on willpower or therapy.

Fortunately, there are a lot of tools out there that can make it possible for you to limit your ability to have cash. You can get a credit card that doesn't work in casinos, you can have a close friend handle your bank accounts, you can hire a trusted payee, you can buy a timed safe, and you can voluntarily exclude yourself from all the nearby casinos. If you have the strength and commitment, it is theoretically possible to make it so you can never have cash in your pocket.

Theoretically possible, yes, but unlikely. We addicted gamblers, when we are in heat, seem always to be able to find a way to acquire cash. We will use pawn shops, steal, embezzle, and borrow (while lying) from friends. Please understand what financial controls can and can't do. They *can* help you to resist or postpone a trip to the casino, "Damn...my husband's wallet has only thirty-five dollars in it, not enough...". They can limit the amount of damage you incur when you do go to the casino, "Sorry sir, this credit card will not work here."

But, if financial controls are your only plan, or the primary plan that you have for treating your addiction, not only will this probably not work, you might be setting yourself or your loved one up for even more serious trouble. If the addict feels the need to gamble strongly enough, *and* if the addict does not have any other tools to fight that powerful urge except a temporary lack of cash, guess what they will do? My guess is they will "get cash" by whatever means they can.

"Get cash" is then down to theft, pawn shops, borrowing, or some other illegal and dangerous thing. The point I'm trying to make is that you should never rely on financial controls *alone* to stop you from gambling. Think of them as a secondary tool, like getting good exercise, or meditation. They can help by putting up barriers that can cause you to pause, and then be able to work on your "urge warfare" skills, or they can simply give you more time and separation from your urge. But in the end, they are unlikely to stop an addicted gambler with an overwhelming urge to gamble and with no skills to fight that urge. The addiction will find a way.

Financial controls are distinct from the other methods described in this book, as they are imposed from the outside. For that reason, they are often recommended early on for those gamblers who are being assisted or guided by a significant other. Once the spouse discovers that they are living with an addicted gambler (who has gambled away a good portion of their money), they will need to protect themselves (and their family) from further losses.

When the magnitude of these losses by the addict is discovered, the spouse, or partner, or parent, or whoever else is vulnerable to losing their own money because of the addicted loved one, needs to take actions immediately. The NCPG website has an excellent section on all the precautions a loved one needs to take to segregate and protect their assets from the gambler (see the references section at the end of the book). If you are in that "significant other" category, do not be shy about doing this. Do not feel guilty about imposing financial controls and protection for yourself and family, you are doing the addict a favor, and maybe even saving their life.

As we addicted gamblers plunge into our addiction, and as we see and know how much financial damage we are doing to our family and friends, our despair, shame, and guilt multiply. All too often this leads to suicidal thoughts and actions. Therefore, the sooner you can keep family assets safe from the gambler, the less likely you will have to deal with the horrifying aftermath of their deaths.

If you are the significant other, there is one more thing you should do - check carefully to see if the addict has taken out, or recently increased, a life insurance policy. If they have, then you know what that means. They are considering (or planning) a suicide. You must figure out an appropriate way to intervene. I can't help you with that - just get help from a therapist, loved one, priest, and do whatever you can (quickly) in a thoughtful way that won't make things worse.

Please though, do not take my concerns about financial controls to mean as an indication that you should ignore them. Like everything else in this book, they can have great value when combined with everything else in this book. Do them all; that is the point.

Okay then, here are a list of actions that you, the addicted gambler, can take to control your ability have cash:

First, some simple things

Keep your bank account balance as low as you can. Have your paycheck automatically deposited and then set up automatic payment of all your bills for the day after the deposit. The sooner you pay your bills, the better.

Make a larger deposit to your 401k every month - 401k money is not readily accessible to you.

If you have a debit card, reduce the amount you can take out from an ATM on any day to 20 or 40 dollars.

Restricted Credit cards

One of the big problems for addicted gamblers is the easy ability to get cash advances at the casino using your standard credit card. Nerdwallet.com has a good summary of the various credit card provider's policies on limiting cash advances. Several companies let you reduce the amount to as little as 100 dollars.

Even if you do lower your cash advance limit there is a loophole with most cards that will let you easily raise the limit back up to the maximum. I know because I've done it too many times to count. On the back of each card is a phone number to call for various emergencies or questions. If you call that number, they will raise your limit back up to the maximum - it takes about 5 minutes, and the funds are available immediately. The credit card companies cannot or will not change that process ability. I even had them put a note on my account to not let me raise my limit, citing that I was a problem gambler. A few months later I decided to try and raise my limit again, and they were again able to do it in just a few minutes, completely ignoring the note.

The American Express card eliminates cash advances altogether. Instead, they allow you to get cash at any ATM with a PIN. Here is an idea: Perhaps you could get an American Express card and then have a significant other set up the pin in secret so that you don't know the PIN. In that way you can have access to a good credit card but without the ability to get cash with it.

The Apple Card does not allow cash advances or ATM withdrawal. The only restriction is that you must have an iPhone. It works with Apple Pay and Apple Wallet, which gives you excellent software support for budgeting, usage reports, etc. If you are an iPhone user, it would be a good choice.

The strongest and most restricted credit card option is the reloadable True Link Next Step Visa Card (www.truelinkfinancial.com). This card is completely customizable, allowing restrictions on where and at what time of day it can be used. It is designed to let the addict have access to a credit card, but not be able to use it to fund their addiction. I would suggest that it only be used in partnership with a restricted payee, or a trusted friend who will set up and manage the various restrictions. Obviously, if the addict manages the restrictions, they could be changed at any time. True Link financial also offers fiduciary services that can be of help in managing all the finances of a person in recovery.

However, restricting the ability of the addicted gambler to get funds from a credit card at the casino will not keep them from gambling. They can always get cash earlier in the day from their bank account or use a debit card at the casino. But it will do something *very important*. Often when the problem gambler decides to gamble, they will plan to do it "responsibly". They will get a set amount of cash and intend to leave when that amount is lost. I have used exactly this plan approximately a million times – basically every time I've gone to the casino.

The problem with that plan is that after I've lost my allotted amount, I don't want to quit gambling. By that I mean I *desperately* want to keep playing. I will walk around the casino looking for cash on the floor (you would be surprised how many times I find bills down there), I'll collect two cent tickets until I have enough to get a dollar bill. I'll go out to the car and scrounge for change on the floor or in the ash tray. That's how desperate the addicted gambler gets when they are physically in the casino, staring at the machines, and unable to play because they are out of money.

If I do have any credit cards in my wallet that have available cash advance amounts, I will take that card to the cage and get whatever the maximum allowable cash advance. Often that amount is a thousand or more dollars. This scenario is played out by every addicted slot machine player that I have ever known, over and over again. If I went to the casino with $300 in my pocket, knowing that was all I could afford, by getting an advance I could easily walk out having lost $2,300. It is precisely that unanticipated failure of my plan, that now unmanageable loss, the confusion, shame, and despair of my weakness, that leads to the sudden and unexpected impulse to commit suicide.

This is why restricting cash advances from your credit cards is so important. It won't prevent you from gambling, you must do that work, but it can keep you alive! I can't emphasize this enough. Remember that this book is dedicated to keeping you alive, and *know that* keeping you from getting additional cash, that you can't afford to lose, in the middle of the night, when you have already compromised your brain, will prevent very many of you from seeking out a bridge abutment on that desperate drive home.

Pease do whatever you can to lower your ability to get cash from your cards. Of course, the best solution is to not have any credit cards; just have a debit card with a low balance in the account.

Transaction Exclusion Programs

There is another little known but effective procedure for limiting your ability to get cash at a casino. You can self-exclude yourself from being able to get a credit card cash advance at a casino by submitting a form to the manufactures of the equipment that authorizes the cash advance. Everi Holdings, Global Payments, and NRT Technologies all offer the ability for you to exclude all your credit cards and bank accounts from working on their equipment.

Each company has a form to fill out where you enter all of your account numbers. Then, when you go to use one of their machines for a withdrawal, you will be declined automatically. The good thing about this concept is that it applies to every casino in the world where those manufacturers have their equipment installed. These three companies probably cover over a thousand casinos or more worldwide.

The forms themselves are hard to find on their websites; in some cases, you may have to call the manufactures in order to get them. I've included the URLs for the forms in the references section of this book, but they may change over time. Even though they may require a little work to locate them, it is well worth doing.

Credit card advances at the casino are perhaps the biggest indicator that you have a serious gambling addiction. They are the last resort to get cash after you have spent the money you brought with you, then maxed out your debit card at the ATM, then cashed checks and emptied your checking account. They are stupidly expensive; the immediate fees are around ten percent of the amount of the advance you requested. You are now gambling with other people's money – essentially a loan at over 24% annual interest rate.

Why would anyone be that stupid, you ask. I can't answer that, but those of you who have been there and done that understand; the rest of you don't. At the point where you decide to get that advance, you have already been gambling for hours. Your brain is officially scrambled. But this is the part that you non-addicts cannot relate to: After the money is gone, the addict is overwhelmingly desperate to keep gambling. The brain juices are flowing. You are in the casino, you have made the drive, you have broken all the barriers you have put up to protect yourself, you have already been gambling for hours, and now you are staring at the machine you were just playing. And you are certain that your machine is about to pay off, big time. But most of all, you just want to keep playing. You *must keep playing!* And the only thing you need is more money.

So, you tip your chair forward to keep others from stealing your machine, and you hustle over to the device that authorizes a credit card advance. You figure out how much cash you might be able to get, and you go up to the cage where the casino guy hands over the last bit of money that you have access to.

Then, after several more hours of messing-up-your-brain button-pushing, you stand up, broke, despairing, angry, disoriented, and you stumble out to your car. This is the moment when the impulse to commit suicide washes over you. This is the moment I've asked you all to prepare for. The cash advance is all too often the tipping point.

Every therapist should have copies of the cash advance exclusion forms at hand, and they should insist that every addicted gambler that they treat fill them out and send them in. Understand, the card holder can still get cash advances at their bank, they just can't get them at a casino in the middle of the night.

Every website that deals with gambling addiction should have a direct link to these forms so that people can download and print them themselves. Every GA meeting should provide them to everyone in attendance. The NCPG legislative agenda should include making access to this process as easy and foolproof as possible. Doing this one simple thing can save lives; hundreds, perhaps thousands every year! So do it.

How about a safe with a timer?

Over the years I've suggested this idea to dozens of people as something that needs to be invented and marketed to the problem gambling community. I can't tell you how many times I have wished I had one.

Now I do! You can find the kSafe at their website (thekitchensafe.com) or on Amazon. The feature that differentiates the kSafe from all other timed safes is that there is *no override*. If you set the timer for three days, put your credit cards and excess cash into it, you absolutely cannot have access to them for three days, unless you take a sledgehammer to it.

The cost is negligible (under $100), so it seems like a reasonable thing to buy. I use it when my friends and family are going away for a while because I know at some point I'll get an urge and there will be fewer outside barrios to prevent me from going. The only drawback is that it is easily broken into; you don't need dynamite or a professional safecracker, you just need a hammer. I'd like to see someone make a much stronger and smaller (just wallet/credit card size) version, even if it cost a little more. It does at least provide one more obstacle, one more hurdle to overcome, and that alone will prevent many trips to the casino.

I have also found the kSafe it to be very effective in the early stages of fighting off an urge. On those days when I have unscheduled time, some money available to me, and no one that I need to lie to to go gamble, I know that an urge is coming and realize it will be getting stronger. I will have to fight it off all day long. I hate those days of mental warfare with my addiction. They are exhausting. So...I've learned to put my cards and checkbook into the kSafe early in the day while I'm still have some willpower. I set the safe for 12 or 24 hours – whatever is necessary to get me past the opportunity to gamble. And then something magical happens (it was totally unexpected the first time I did this). The urge simply vanishes – poof! It's gone. For the rest of the day I don't think about gambling because my addiction knows it is now impossible to do. Kenny slinks back into his stinking hole.

Another use: If you somehow find yourself with a large amount of cash (I won't ask where it came from), and you won't be going to your bank to deposit it for a day or more, simply drop it in the safe and set the timer for when you will be going to the bank. Once again, temptation removed. There are many other things you can do with this safe as well: car keys, brownies, cigarettes, etc. It is a useful device, get one.

Representative Payee

It is possible to turn over all your finances to a third party who will receive your paycheck, pay your bills and then give you a small allowance for spending money each week. This person or company is called a "Representative Payee". Representative payees are most often used for the elderly who are no longer able to handle their own finances. The payee can either be an individual who you know and trust, or a third-party individual, or a company. The Social Security Administration has a significant amount of information available on this process. Just go to their website and search on "representative payee".

An organizational payee is a company that handles your finances. You can find some information on organizational payees at crisscross.org, a large non-profit who offers payee services, including those for addicted gamblers. I've never used a payee, or known anyone who has, so I can't vouch for the process, or how much it costs, or even the integrity of the companies who offer those services. You will have to do that research yourself.

A seemingly reasonable compromise to a professional payee is to have a significant other, a relative, or a close friend manage the gamblers finances. They probably won't charge anything, and they can be more flexible if necessary. Unfortunately, pitfalls abound with this plan. Us addicted gamblers are experts at lying and deception. If faced with a choice of going gambling when we really want to or lying to a friend - we will lie. So unless you want to put yourself in a position where you will likely lie and deceive a close friend or relative, I suggest you leave them out of this process entirely.

Online gambling exclusion software

As Sheryl Anderson from Vanguard Center for Gambling Recovery pointed out in her foreword to this book, we are on the verge of an online gambling tsunami. Many states are rushing to legalize online sports betting and online slots, and many other online games with a betting component. Even scarier, online betting laws are becoming irrelevant as technologies have emerged to simply bypass those laws.

This new explosion of online gambling opportunities is just beginning. You can be certain that now that online betting is accessible by everyone, the gaming industry's "creative juices" will be flowing. They will invent new and exciting opportunities. Things like totally different games not based on the slot machine paradigm, and adding betting opportunities to traditional video games, and who knows what else. As I write this paragraph (03/2021) the Top Shot NBA NFT lottery has exploded (nuff said about that...total craziness). The point is: The sky (or the gutter) is the limit for online opportunities for you to gamble away your money.

During the pandemic of 2020-2021 online slots were a safe option to avoid infection and along with casinos being closed, they became the dominate slot machine option. Many more people became addicted. The result of being able to gamble with slot machines from the convenience of home is going to addict millions more, especially younger people more comfortable with the online world.

The temptation to gamble online is so easy to give into – you don't have to get dressed, get cash, drive to the casino, or even let your partner or family know that you are gambling – the casino has come to you! You get an urge, and three seconds later you are gambling!

If the online world is now the problem, perhaps it can also provide the solution. Many software companies are now selling programs that will effectively block your devices from even getting to the gambling websites.

Ivan Jenic has written a good article about the choices for software programs that block access to virtually all opportunities to gamble online (search on "windows report block gambling ivan jenic" to read the article). I have installed on my computer one of these programs named Gamban. It appears to me to be comprehensive. I can't get to any slot machine sites, even the free play ones. It stops fantasy sports, poker sites, and even the Powerball site.

Here is a tip: You cannot uninstall Gamban until your contract with them expires. They give you a choice of monthly payments or annual payments, so pay for the entire year and then you can't rescind it for a year. The cost is minimal, especially when you compare it to all of the money you will save.

Casino Voluntary Exclusion Programs

Voluntary exclusions programs make it possible for a person to voluntarily ban him or herself from a casino as a way to deal with their gambling problem. In some states these programs are required by law to be available, and most casinos do it to comply with the code of ethics of the American Gaming Association. I would be surprised if any large casino did not offer this option.

The way this works is that you must go to the casino and speak to the security people. They will provide a form that requires you to fill out some standard info, and then they will take one or several photos of you. States and casinos vary as to the specific terms and conditions. The biggest variable is the length of the ban. Often it is an irrevocable lifetime ban (the best option). It can also be as short as a one-year ban, but in that case, it will automatically renew every year for one additional year, so you don't have to do anything to keep it in force. In order to stop it from renewing you must send them a letter or go back to the casino and cancel the ban.

When the ban is in force several things happen. If they spot you in the casino, you will likely be escorted out if it is your first offence. If you are a repeat offender, they have the right to have you arrested for trespassing. In some cases, or some casinos, they may have you arrested on the first offence. It's probably not worth the risk to find out what is their actual policy.

Obviously, you could put on a disguise, but even then, with the sophistication of current facial-recognition software, you could get caught. But if you do sneak in and gamble for a while, when they do catch you, they will confiscate your ticket. And if you should be fortunate enough to win a hand-pay jackpot, you will have to quickly walk away from the machine because hand-pays require you to identify yourself. And because you can't identify yourself, you won't be able to get cash from the cage. The exclusion agreement also stops the casino from sending you promotional material in the mail or email and it cancels your loyalty program membership. Please take a friend, a spouse, or someone who will prevent you from gambling when you go to each casino to fill out the paperwork.

In some ways, the decision to voluntarily exclude yourself from all the casinos in your area is a litmus test as to how committed you are to your recovery. By doing this, you can be proud of yourself and encouraged that you can stop gambling. It is a very positive step. Do it. You are worth it!

I will repeat my advice about financial controls in general. If these restrictions are imposed on the gambler without any additional treatment efforts, it could lead to serious problems - if the compulsive gambler desperately wants to keep gambling, and they are cut off from their own funds, they may resort to more drastic means. The options then become pawn shops, stealing, embezzlement, even bank robbery (I've been in treatment (or meetings) with two bank robbers). When imposing financial controls from the outside, just make sure that the gambler is in some frame of mind where they are not in denial, and they are *wanting* to stop gambling, and are willing to cooperate and able to put in the effort necessary to make it happen.

Chapter 15

Odds and Endings

I have several additional ideas that might be of help to you, but I couldn't figure out how to make them long enough for their own chapter. Here they are, in no particular order:

Move

If you lived on an island in the middle of the Pacific Ocean with no casinos, I'm guessing that you wouldn't be able to gamble – problem solved! And to your great good fortune, there is a very nice Pacific Island chain that has no slot machines or casinos at all: Hawaii! I know it is a bit expensive, but if you add up all the money you slip into those evil machines, maybe it would be cheaper to live there. Think of that, moving to Hawaii to save money!

There is one other state that bans casinos and gambling of all flavors. Utah is casino free, but it does share a long border with Nevada, so I'm afraid your good intentions would simply result in long road trips.

Several years ago, after my first stint at Vanguard, I moved to Friday Harbor in the San Juan Islands of Washington state. The ferry to the mainland sailed only a few times a day, took several hours, and required that a reservation be made ahead of time. Friday Harbor is a beautiful place to live, and I enjoyed my two years spent there. My gambling never completely stopped, as trips to the mainland were inevitable, but it was significantly curtailed. The result was less gambling and a beautiful place to live, a win-win.

I'm sure that there are many other remote and interesting places around the country that are far from casinos that you might consider. But like the caution about financial controls being the only hammer on your belt, relying solely on remoteness as your only hope to stop gambling won't work. There will always be opportunities to go somewhere where the machines are patiently waiting for you and your addiction. But again, when used with all the other ideas in this book, getting as far away as possible from the casinos will certainly create a strong barrier.

Hypnosis

I am very interested in the potential of hypnosis to alter our thinking about slot machines. Wouldn't it be cool if someone could hypnotize you and convince you that you *hate* slot machines with a passion? I've tried to find examples of the use of hypnosis for compulsive gambling, but I have found nothing. I called a couple of hypno-therapists to see if they knew of any ideas about treating addicted gamblers, but they also had no knowledge of that possibility. I think someone should do a study of this idea.

I have read a little about self-hypnosis that was interesting and might be applicable. As you go to sleep at night, during the last few minutes before you drift off, you are apparently in a very suggestable state. If you plan ahead to make yourself repeat some idea, it can be similar to having that idea planted during hypnosis. I have tried at various times to tell myself phrases such as: "I won't gamble tomorrow", or "I hate slot machines". Unfortunately, there is no way to know if that works. Still, there is no reason not to try it, it is an easy thing to do.

Get a dog

If you have a pet at home that needs your attention every few hours, guess what? You can't stay at the casino for any extended periods unless you want to clean up messes or replace destroyed furniture.

Loneliness and boredom are often given as a reason to go gambling. Dogs can help ease both of those, and you will probably be generally happier with a nice dog on your lap! I don't think cats would have the same effect (full disclosure: I don't like cats).

Medications

The therapeutic community frequently states that addicted gamblers also suffer from other disorders such as depression, alcohol addiction or drug addiction. I don't know if compulsive gamblers actually experience those problems at a higher rate than the general population, or whether the therapeutic community notices it more because they only have information from those people who present themselves for treatment.

There is a chicken and egg problem with gamblers and depression: do they gamble because they are depressed, or are they depressed because they gamble? No matter, if you are depressed perhaps an anti-depressant may help you. See a doctor or someone who can determine an appropriate treatment. And if you see someone, be sure to tell them about your gambling problem. They need to know that. Unload that secret.

There is a category of drugs that can increase your urge to gamble. Not surprisingly it has to do with dopamine. The dopaminergic medications used commonly for Parkinson's disease cause people to want to gamble. If you are on those drugs and gambling excessively, talk to your doctor about your gambling, he might be able to find other medication options.

I've found only one medication that some therapists or researchers are experimenting with to treat gambling addiction. Naltrexone hydrochloride, widely used as an opioid antagonist, in several studies has been shown to reduce urges to gamble. And since it is used commonly for opioid and alcohol addiction, perhaps your doctor may think it would also be right for use with your gambling addiction. There is no widespread consensus that using Naltrexone for gambling addiction is helpful. There need to be more trials and controlled studies. And, please understand that I am way outside my pay grade by discussing medication in this paragraph, so talk to your therapist or doctor if this or any other medication is of interest to you.

Harm Reduction

Harm reduction comes in two flavors regarding gambling addiction. First flavor: It is used to describe the industry-wide actions that can be taken by the casino owners, equipment manufacturers, and government agencies to limit the damage done by the addicted gambler while playing. There are dozens of ideas floating around that could make a difference. Some of these ideas will be completely understood by the gambler but may seem fairly benign to the general public. For example, the casinos could shut off each machine for 15 minutes after 45 minutes of continuous play. It might seem as though that would not be a major imposition on the average player as they could just go to another machine. However, the compulsive slot player very often sits at the same machine for hours, sometimes days! Either the machine is paying, or they fervently believe it is about to start paying. For them, having to get up and start a new machine breaks the spell. If it is automatically turned off, they may just get up and leave.

Other ideas are to limit the highest amount you can bet on any spin to one dollar, or to eliminate the ability of the player to stop the reels early, or after a certain amount of loss during continuous play the machine would send you a message asking you to consider your limit for that day.

These are all excellent suggestions. Unfortunately, none of them will ever be adopted. Various estimates put the amount of profit that a casino derives from problem gamblers at 60 to 70 percent. While the casinos will express concern for problem gamblers as fellow human beings who suffer from gambling addiction, there is no way they are ever going to screw with that very significant revenue stream.

The second flavor of harm reduction are ideas for the gambler to continue to gamble, but reduce the damage done to themselves and their loved ones to an acceptable level. Many of the ideas in this book fall into that category. Self-transaction-exclusion for credit card advances does that. Moving far away from a casino would do that. I recommend doing all these things. Reducing harm is a good thing. But never make reducing harm your ultimate goal. Gamblers Anonymous has it right when they say that addicted gambling is a progressive disease. As long as the addiction monkey is in your head, you will continue to gamble more often and for bigger bets.

The goal should always be long-term abstinence. The benefit of long-term abstinence that I desire the most, even more than financial stability, is to get that monkey out of my head. I want to stop thinking about avoiding gambling, or deceitfully planning to go gambling, or feeling the shame and despair of having just gone gambling. I want to eliminate *forever* those depressing thoughts. Please don't stop at reducing harm. Go all the way to permanent sobriety. Send the monkey away.

Commitments

I think the therapeutic community would point out many unintended negative consequences about this idea, but I think it could help if used appropriately. My good friend who has 44 years of sobriety calls these commitments "stakes in the ground". The more stakes you have, the more things you can grab on to when the world sends you a shitstorm. One of the therapists that I have seen over the years did this: At the end of each session she asked me to commit to her that I would not gamble during the next week. I appreciated that she asked me that, and I committed to her that I would. It became something that I tried to do simply because she had asked me.

The unintended risks occurred when I did gamble. My choices at the next session with her were these: Either I could lie to her (not a good idea to lie to your therapist), or I would feel defeated and shameful admitting to her that I gambled after I promised her that I wouldn't. From the therapist's point of view, that is probably not what they want for their patient. I guess that is why the other seven therapists never asked me for that commitment.

You could make a commitment not to gamble to people other than your therapist. Of course, when a significant other becomes aware of your gambling, you will use that promise as your first option, even though you have no idea if you can follow through. This can then become a likely starting point for even more lies and deception. At this early stage, be cautious about telling your partner you won't do it again, because the odds are you will. Instead, say you will promise to get help. Then get help.

Perhaps at some point in your recovery you might begin to feel confident that you are winning the battle with your addiction. At that point it might be helpful to put some additional stakes in the ground. Talk to a close friend, tell them what you have been going through. Share with them how hard it has been and perhaps ask for their help as you continue to fight for a gambling-free life. Whenever you see them ask them to ask you if you have gambled recently. The more commitments you make, the more you will not want to disappoint. Stakes in the ground.

The Twelfth Step

*"Having had a spiritual awakening as the result of these
steps, we tried to carry this message to other addicts, and to
practice these principles in all our affairs."*
The Twelfth Step of the AA program

*"Practical experience shows that nothing will so much insure
immunity from drinking as intensive work with other
alcoholics. It works when other activities fail. This is our
twelfth suggestion: Carry this message to other alcoholics!
You can help when no one else can. You can secure their
confidence when others fail. Remember they are very ill.*

*Life will take on new meaning. To watch people recover, to
see them help others, to watch loneliness vanish, to see a
fellowship grow up about you, to have a host of friends - this
is an experience you must not miss. We know you will not
want to miss it. Frequent contact with newcomers and with
each other is the bright spot of our lives."*
From the AA Big Book, Chapter 7, pg. 89

Much has been written about the twelfth step in the AA 12-step program. I don't presume to be able to add anything meaningful to that vast library of analysis and thought. For those not familiar, it goes like this: As your recovery progresses, the time comes when you need to get out of your own head and go out and help others. By helping others, you will take your own recovery to a new level. You can then feel pride and meaning in your life by using your suffering to enlighten and reduce the suffering in others like yourself. It is powerful stuff. Go to the internet and read all about it.

You can become a sponsor in GA. You can advocate to your state or national representatives for "harm reduction" policies and legislation. You can write a blog or contribute to an online support group. You can join NCPG and contribute to their activities. Use your imagination - just go out and do something. By doing this, your losses, your shame and guilt, your negative experiences, can all become a source of something good. You will feel great about your efforts to help others.

This book is my twelfth step, and I have loved doing it. My great fantasy is that it gets published and is read by millions of people – addicts and therapists. My greater fantasy is that it saves thousands of lives. Imagine how wonderful that would be!

Perhaps this next suggestion is too blatant. It is likely that the publisher will have it removed, though I hope not. Remember that the specific purpose of this book is to prevent addicted gamblers from committing suicide. Remember that it is likely that over ten thousand suffering gamblers did commit suicide last year. Blatant or not, here goes: You can help save those lives. Make this your twelfth step: provide a copy of this book to the people who need it. Give a copy to everyone in your GA group. Provide several copies to your therapist so she can give them to her other patients. Send a copy to all your state legislators so they can see how their greed for campaign funds hurts so many of their constituents. Do whatever you can to get this book in the hands of those ten thousand who are now on track to commit suicide next year! If a great many of you do this, many lives will be saved. You will have participated in one hell of a twelfth step!

Endings

For those of you who are problem gamblers on the road to recovery, thank you for reading this book! I hope it has given you renewed hope for a gambling-free life. However, I'm sorry to say that even if this looks like your lesson is about to end, you would be wrong. You have one more assignment, one more chapter that you must read. Go back now and reread chapter two -*Please don't kill yourself today*.

Relearn the precautionary steps I recommended in that chapter. Promise yourself (and me) that you will do the work suggested in that chapter. Promise that you will commit to doing those steps and practicing those steps as often as you can. Promise yourself and everyone who loves you that you will do those things.

Make that promise so that you won't become one of next year's ten thousand. Make that promise right now. Do it! You are worth it!

The End.

Notes and References

Introduction

General Information About Gambling Addiction

References

Books:

Addiction by Design 2012, Princeton University Press
Natasha Dow Schull
Exhaustive analysis of how slot machines are designed to addict the players. Like much of the literature about slot machine gambling, it is already a bit dated, but for those interested in understanding how the gaming industry is out to addict you, it is a must read.

Videos:

Sixty Minutes segment on slot machines 2011 Lesley Stall
You Tube search terms: *slot machines the big gamble*

Natasha Schull is featured again in this overview of the epidemic of slot machine addiction. Amazing how most of the videos available on slot machines are already out of date.

Articles and Websites:

The Atlantic, December 2016, "How Casinos Enable Gambling Addicts" John Rosengren
Web search terms: **the Atlantic losing it all**
https://www.theatlantic.com/magazine/archive/2016/12/losing-it-all/505814/

This is the best article to read for an overview of slot machine addiction and the awful consequences. Long, but well researched.

Mayo Clinic Compulsive Gambling

Web Search terms: **mayo clinic 2016 compulsive gambling**

https://www.mayoclinic.org/diseases-conditions/compulsive-gambling/symptoms-causes/syc-20355178

Basic clinical description of compulsive gambling

Chapter 1

Let's Talk About Suicide

References

Books:

Suicidal, why we kill ourselves Jesse Bering,
University of Chicago press, 2018
The best current book on suicide written by a talented
researcher and writer.
Quote: "Never kill yourself while you are suicidal".

*How I stayed alive while my brain was trying to kill
me* Susan Rose Blauner, Harper Collins, 2002
A personal journey through suicide country with
emphasis on seeking help.
Quote: "To get help, you have to ask for it."

DSM-5 American Psychiatric Publishing 2013
For those that do not know - the DSM is (from
Wikipedia): *The **Diagnostic Manual of Mental
Disorders** (DSM), published by the American Psychiatric
Association (APA), it offers a common language and
standard criteria for the classification of mental disorders.*
Pages 585 to 589 deal with gambling addiction.

Quote: "Gambling disorder is more prevalent among first-degree relatives of people with moderate to severe alcohol use disorder" (count me in).

Articles and Websites:

CDC Current Trends Operational Criteria for Determining Suicide (from the CDC) Web search terms: current trends for determining suicide
https://www.cdc.gov/mmwr/preview/mmwrhtml/0000
1318.htm
This is the article quoted from in chapter 1

Quote: "No explicit criteria exist to assist in determining whether a death is a suicide."

Quick Facts About Gambling and Suicide (from New Jersey council on Compulsive Gambling's Website - 800-gambler)

Web search terms: 800gambler quick facts suicide
https://800gambler.org/quick-facts-gambling-suicide/

This article documents data related to compulsive gambling suicides from various sources around the country. Alarming, but outdated (from 2010).

Quote: "In Gulfport, Mississippi, suicides increased by 213 percent (from 24 to 75) in the first two years after casinos arrived. In neighboring Biloxi, suicide attempts jumped by 1,000 percent (from 6 to 66) in the first year alone".

Quote: "There is no Way to explain it to you if you are not living in our personal hell, because we don't understand it either"

Problem gamblers much more likely to attempt suicide (from *The Guardian*)

Web search terms: **Guardian problem gamblers more likely suicide**

Cites one of the few studies of the potential of compulsive gamblers to commit suicide.

Quote: "Research commissioned by a leading UK gambling charity, GambleAware, found that problem gamblers were six times more likely than alcohol or drug abusers to have suicidal thoughts or try to take their own life – and could be 15 times more likely to do so."

Facts and Statistics (from the American Association of Suicidology website)

Web Search terms: **suicidology facts and statistics**

An organization dedicated to creating awareness and prevention about suicide in general (though nothing discussed about gambling related suicide) the fact sheet referenced above has good basic statistics.

Quote: "Each suicide resulted in 135 people exposed (knew the person). Each suicide affects a large circle of people, who may be in need of clinician services or support following exposure."

Chapter 2

Please Don't Kill Yourself Today
(You can always do it tomorrow)

References

Books:

The 5 Second Rule Mel Robbins, Savio Republic Publishing, 2017

There is a lot more to "The 5 Second Rule" than what I referred to in Chapter 2 (the starting ritual). There is a whole book in fact. As is the case with many of the ideas in this book, it can be useful in your life in general.

Quote: "I want you to have a massive breakthrough, right now. As in, right-right now."

Articles and Websites:

How the brain gets addicted to gambling (from Scientific American, 2013)
Web search terms: **scientific american 2013 brain gambling**
https://www.scientificamerican.com/article/how-the-brain-gets-addicted-to-gambling/

Basic overview on brain chemistry in Problem Gamblers.

Quote: "Addictive drugs and gambling rewire neural circuits in similar ways."

Has dopamine got us hooked on tech? (from The Guardian, 2018)

Web search terms: **Guardian dopamine facebook addiction**

https://www.theguardian.com/technology/2018/mar/04/has-dopamine-got-us-hooked-on-tech-facebook-apps-addiction

A good explanation of the relationship between dopamine and addiction - including addiction to Facebook and other apps.

Quote: "Unnaturally large rewards are not filtered in the brain – they go directly into the brain and overstimulate, which can generate addiction. When that happens, we lose our willpower."

Chapter 3

Detox

References

Articles and Websites:

Signs and Symptoms of Gambling Withdrawal (from Algamus.org website)
Web search terms: **Algamus symptoms of gambling withdrawal**
https://www.algamus.org/blog/signs-and-symptoms-of-gambling-withdrawal

Overview of the symptoms and duration of gambling withdrawal.
Quote: "The gambling withdrawal period often results in a flood of symptoms that can result in extreme emotional lows."

Stimulant Withdrawal and Detox (from the Addiction Center website)
Web search terms: **stimulant withdrawal and detox**
https://www.addictioncenter.com/stimulants/withdrawal-and-detox/

This is an excellent overview of stimulant (cocaine, meth, amphetamines, etc.) withdrawal symptoms and timelines. Many gambling therapists (and me too) believe gambling withdrawal symptoms (primarily slot machine gambling) are very similar to stimulant withdrawal.
Quote: "The psychological withdrawal from stimulants can be especially severe, leading some former users to relapse, others may even become suicidal or violent."

Dopamine Deficiency: What you need to know (from Medicalnewstoday website)
Web search terms: **Dopamine deficiency**
https://www.medicalnewstoday.com/articles/320637.php

I believe that during withdrawal, slot machine addicts experience dopamine deficiency in the same way that drug abusers do during withdrawal (disclaimer: there is no data/study/literature that asserts (or denies) this. My opinion only.). This article explains all the aspects of dopamine deficiency.
Quote: "Supplements to boost levels of vitamin D, magnesium, and omega-3 essential fatty acids may also help to raise dopamine levels, but there needs to be more research into whether this is effective. Activities that make a person feel happy and relaxed are also thought to increase dopamine levels. These may include exercise, therapeutic massage, and meditation."

Chapter 4

Do You Want A future?

References

Books:

A Day at a time Anonymous, Hazelden Publishing, 1976
The daily reflection and prayer books are a staple of most recovery programs. This one is one of the originals published by Hazelden for Gamblers Anonymous almost fifty years ago. Best bargain is to buy it used from Amazon. This version is very higher-power based, but if you do a general search for a daily meditation book, you will find every possible philosophy represented – from Stoic to Taoist, and everything else. I think these books are a helpful way to start your day with your recovery in mind. After all, recovery is forever, you need all the help you can get.

Chicken soup for the recovering soul Primary authors are Jack Caufield and Mark Victor Hansen, with help from many others, Health Communications Inc., 1998
I'm sure everyone is familiar with these books. This one is specifically for people in recovery. Focused on alcohol abuse and some drug abuse, so I found only a few of the stories to be helpful. Still, recovery is forever, this could be helpful to some of you. Again, find it used on Amazon.

Videos:

Here is my strong recommendation regarding You Tube videos that interview recovering gamblers: **STAY AWAY FROM THEM.** Many of them use footage of slot machines as an intro to the video, and my belief is that none of them are very helpful. But the main reason to avoid them is that (for me at least) they are triggers, they generate immediate urges. Not worth it. Don't do it.

Articles and Websites:

Daily Inspirational Messages
Web search terms: **daily inspiration messages**
Once again, there are maybe hundreds of choices of places that will send you an upbeat daily message. Be a little careful of who you choose, many are not reputable. Zig Zigler said this: "People often say that motivation doesn't last. Well, neither does bathing – that's why we recommend it daily."

Chapter 5

First Step - Therapy

References

Videos:

How to Seek Therapy
YouTube search terms: **how to seek therapy**
https://www.youtube.com/watch?v=cDoaQIQZU1k

Brief, simple, basic instruction on how to find a therapist. Worth 5 minutes of your time if you are trying to decide to start therapy.

Gambling Disorder and Suicide Ideation Ohio
YouTube search terms: **gambling suicide ideation**
https://www.youtube.com/watch?v=Y7u7TeucSQM

Good overview, a little long. Intended for therapists in order to get them to understand the danger of suicides in problem gamblers and the imperative to explore suicide with their addicted gambling patients.

Articles and Websites:

You should see someone, a guide to doing therapy,
Yukai Du, Huffpost Wellness Series

Web search terms: **huffpost you should see someone**
https://www.huffpost.com/feature/you-should-see-someone#masthead

Excellent series of articles on why anyone who is dealing with mental/personality issues should seek therapy. The series covers everything you would like to know about therapy. Literally over a dozen articles - **highly recommended!**

Quote: "We want to normalize therapy and show you how to do it within your own life and budget. That's why we've launched "You Should See Someone," a guide that will teach you everything you need to know about doing therapy. The series is packed with informative, no-B.S. stories on how to seek help and embrace it once you do. Because you SHOULD see someone if you need to — and there shouldn't be anything preventing you from that."

American Psychological Association Website
Web search terms: **apa.org choose therapist**
https://www.apa.org/helpcenter/choose-therapist

The APA (American Psychological Association) is one of the largest national groups for professional psychologists and researchers. They have many articles that can be of value
to you on this site. This article is good basic info about how to choose a someone to work with.

Chapter 6

Gamblers Anonymous

References

Videos:

What it's like to attend your first GA Meeting, After Gambling Podcast
YouTube search terms: **after gambling podcast gss 008**
https://www.youtube.com/watch?v=-Mkd_K71Pfc

Clear, simple, 15 minute talk about what to expect when going to your first GA meeting

What are the twelve steps (simplified), Sober Grid
You Tube search terms: **the twelve steps simplified**
https://www.youtube.com/watch?v=5FpMs8gXRkw

Short (6 min.) explanation of the 12 steps (the non-god version)

Articles and Websites:

The Gamblers Anonymous Website
http://www.gamblersanonymous.org/ga/

Gamblers Anonymous organizations website. Use this to find a meeting near you. Look up the 20 questions test here. Then take it.

The top ten reasons people drop out of Gamblers Anonymous, Northstar Problem Gambling Alliance Web search terms: northstar gambling top ten reasons https://northstarproblemgambling.org/2013/12/top-ten-reasons-that-people-drop-out-of-the-gamblers-anonymous-program/

Good info on what to set for realistic expectations for your GA meeting, and why to keep attending when you are unsure.

Quote: "Every GA meeting has someone that seems to rub us the wrong way. Things are going to be said that upset us. Don't allow comments to keep you from coming back. Remember, principles before personalities."

The Irrationality of Alcoholics Anonymous, Atlantic Magazine, Gabriell Glaser, Atlantic Magazine, 2015
Web search terms: atlantic irrationality of aa
https://www.theatlantic.com/magazine/archive/2015/0
4/the-irrationality-of-alcoholics-anonymous/386255/

A strong condemnation of AA and the twelve-step program. As I've mentioned before, there is no magic pill for solving addiction. And that includes GA and the twelve steps. It is what it is, and if it doesn't work for you - so be it. There is no need to feel guilty about you not liking it or not using it.

Chapter 7

Inpatient Programs

References

Videos:

Outpatient Treatment Vs. Inpatient Treatment: The Clearing NW, Friday Harbor Washington
YouTube search terms: **theclearingnw outpatient inpatient an honest comparison**
https://www.youtube.com/watch?v=q2Llj2Om6QM

A two minute video discussing the pros and cons of inpatient vs. outpatient treatment. Very basic, but mercifully short.

Gambling treatment inpatient, Luna Moody
YouTube search terms: **luna moody gambling treatment inpatient**
https://www.youtube.com/watch?v=vvS_hqGvHyw

This is fascinating. If you are considering inpatient treatment, watch all five of her videos form oldest to newest. Heartfelt, compelling, and a little rambling as expected from unscripted monologue. Angie, a self-described compulsive gambler, relates her experiences at the Vanguard treatment facility. I could not have said it better.

The websites of the four dedicated inpatient treatment programs:

Vanguard Center for Gambling recovery at Project Turnabout
Web search terms: **gambling treatment vanguard**
https://www.projectturnabout.org/treatment/gambling-recovery/vanguard/

Granite Falls Minnesota, 20 beds

Louisiana Association on Compulsive Gambling Center of Recovery - CORE
Web search terms: **core gambling recovery louisiana**
http://www.helpforgambling.org/core

Shreveport Louisiana, 21 beds

Bridgeway Recovery Services, Santiam House

Web Search terms: **santiam house salem**
https://bridgewayrecovery.com/treatment_residential_problem_gambling.php

Salem Oregon, 8 beds

Algamus Gambling Treatment Center
Web search terms: **algamus treatment center**
https://www.algamus.org/

Prescott Arizona, 10 beds

Chapter 8

Smart Recovery

References

Videos:

Smart Recovery Videos
YouTube search terms: **smart recovery**
www.youtube.com

There are dozens of videos on YouTube explaining and demonstrating all aspects of Smart Recovery. They are worth watching – you will feel like you know a lot more about addiction after an evening watching these videos.

Articles and Websites:

Smart Recovery website, Self Management and Recovery Training Organization
Web search terms: **smartrecovery.org**
https://www.smartrecovery.org/

This website has all the information that you need to understand Smart Recovery. Follow the links there to find a local meeting, follow the links to the toolbox page for dozens of third-party articles. A wealth of information.

Quote: Our mutual support meetings are free and open to anyone seeking science-based, self-empowered addiction recovery.

Chapter 9

CBT - Cognitive Behavioral Theory

References

Books:

Cognitive Behavioral Theory Basics and Beyond, 2nd edition, 2011, Judith Beck
"The leading text for students and practicing therapists"
Unfortunately, the price ($30 - $50) doesn't work for me, so I can't tell you if it is helpful.

Videos:

CBT Simply Explained
You tube search term: **CBT simply explained**
https://www.youtube.com/watch?v=WhMmZJ3H1E8

This is a four-minute long basic introduction to CBT, worthwhile, well done
There are dozens more CBT videos on you tube - this is the best source for CBT information

Articles and Websites:

Cognitive Behavioral Theory (CBT), Provincial System Support (PSSP), Canada
Web search terms: cbt pssp gambling Ontario

Good overview of how a therapist might use CBT with an addicted gambler. Though, as I said in the chapter on CBT, I believe the CBT therapist should stop claiming that addicted gamblers will somehow be cured when their "faulty thinking" about winning is corrected. The idea that addicted slot machine players don't know that "in the long run" they will loose, is absurd. They know that, but they also know that this time they might actually win. They know that this time they might even win a jackpot. They know this because they have done it many times in the past. That argument may seem logical, but it is simply not persuasive to the addicted gambler.

My belief is that the best way to use CBT with addicted gamblers is to learn how to understand and combat urges.

Chapter 10

Mindfulness

References

Books:

Mindfulness Based Stress Reduction, Lehrhaupt and Meibert, 2017

There are a zillion books now on Mindfulness, this is one that I've read. A good intro into MBSR

Be here now Ram Dass, 1971
Back to the beginning (along with Alan Watts' *The Way of Zen,* 1957) this is where us old folks got our first taste of Zen.

Quote: "No matter how high we got, we always came down." A good reason to choose mindfulness over gambling - you don't come down.

Videos:

Just go to YouTube and search on "Mindfulness". Watch a bunch of them, a good way to spend a rainy afternoon.

Articles and Websites:

www.mindful.org

They have the URL, so they must be important. You will find lots of info, links, books and other good stuff there.

A Web search on Mindfulness will also result in a Web gaggle of places to go.

Chapter 11

DBT - Dialectical Behavioral Theory & Self Compassion

References

Books:

A "DBT" search on Amazon will yield about a dozen books on DBT. Unfortunately, they all seem to be directed to therapists, and they are all too expensive for a patient trying to learn about DBT. So folks, an opportunity. There doesn't seem to be DBT book for the general public.

Videos:

Marsha Linehan, Balancing Acceptance and Change
YouTube search terms: **marsha linehan balancing acceptance and change**
https://www.youtube.com/watch?v=JMUk0TBWASc

Designed primarily for therapists and quite long. Still, it is worth watching Marsha Linehan lecture.

A YouTube search on just "DBT" will provide many 5-minute overviews. Interestingly, they are all very different from each other.

Articles and Websites:

How to Start Healing Emotionally from Gambling Addiction, Headward, Annika Lindberg, 2019
Web Search terms: Headward Annika Lindberg (go to the main site and click on blog content)
https://www.headward.co.uk/blogcontent/2019/7/22/how-to-start-healing-emotionally-from-gambling-addiction-instead-of-continuing-to-self-punish

Excellent article and excellent website. Ms. Lindberg's article and approach operate at the intersection of gambling addiction, DBT's radical acceptance, and CBT's behavioral changes. Everything on this site is worth reading. Highly recommended.

Self-Compassion, Dr. Kristin Neff
Web search terms: **self-compassion**
https://self-compassion.org/

I believe it is very difficult to begin the process of healing and recovery until you have found a way to put your shame, guilt, and self-loathing into the rearview mirror. This is a site that can help you do just that.
Quote: "With self-compassion, we give ourselves the same kindness and care we'd give to a good friend."

Chapter 12

Willpower

References

Books:

Willpower: Rediscovering the greatest human strength, Roy F. Baumeister and John Tierney, Penguin Press, 2011

This book contains everything you need to know about the current understanding of willpower as a force in our lives. Tierney is an excellent writer; the book is both entertaining and informative. Every therapist should have this on their bookshelf.

However, there is also a body of thought that believes Baumeister's theory of willpower being akin to a storage battery (ego depletion) is completely wrong. It seems that so much of psychology is subject to strong disagreement, you wonder if it should be even be called a science.

Videos:

YouTube search on "willpower" will power your day.

Articles and Websites:

What you need to know about Willpower, The American Psychological Association (APA, The APA is the leading scientific and professional organization representing psychology in the United States, with more than 121,000 researchers, educators, clinicians, consultants and students as its members.)
Web search terms: **apa.org willpower**
https://www.apa.org/helpcenter/willpower

Excellent and comprehensive overview of "The psychological science of self-control". The article largely supports Baumeister's theory of ego depletion.

Chapter 13

Urge Warfare

References

Videos:

The Secret to Self-Control, Jonathan Bricker, TedX
Rainier, 2014
YouTube search terms: **self control bricker**
https://www.youtube.com/watch?v=tTb3d5cjSFI

A Must watch. Bricker uses the term "willingness" to
describe a way to fight urges. His "willingness"
concept is similar to mindfulness and especially
Marsha Linehan's radical acceptance from DBT. I use
his example of walking away from the urge – creating
separation from the urge. Watch this video.

Articles and Websites:

*Riding the Wave: Using Mindfulness to Help Cope
With Urges,* Portland Psychotherapy Clinic, 2011
Web search terms: **riding the wave urge surfing**
https://portlandpsychotherapyclinic.com/2011/11/ridin
g-wave-using-mindfulness-help-cope-urges/

A detailed instruction manual for learning mindfulness
urge surfing

Chapter 14

Financial Controls

References

Articles and Websites:

Research on Self Exclusion Programs, NCRG, 2010
Web search terms: **ncrg self exclusion**
https://www.ncrg.org/resources/publications/issues-insights/research-self-exclusion-programs

The National Center for Responsible Gaming (NCRG) is the industry funded lobbying group focused on responsible gaming. As long as you understand that their funding comes from the gambling industry, it is a useful resource. They have several articles about self exclusion on their site (as the self exclusion program is an industry based program).

Self Transaction Exclusion Programs

Below are the three "Transaction" based self exclusion programs from the leaders in cash-advance technology located in casinos. Everi and NRTech provide a printable PDF on their site. Global payments only provides a phone number to call. When you call that number, you get their basic call center. Ask to talk to a supervisor, because the first level call center person does not know about the self exclusion form.

Everi
Web search terms: **everi request to block transactions**
https://www.everi.com/wp-content/uploads/Instruction-to-Reject-Transaction-STEP-20180319-v7.pdf

NRtech
Web search terms: **nrtech exclusion form enrollment**
https://www.nrttech.com/wp-content/uploads/2019/02/Exclusion-Program-Enrollment-Form-Final.pdf

Global Payments
Web search terms: **global payments self exclusion**
https://www.vippreferred.com/en/self-exclusion

KSafe Timed Safe
Web search terms: **ksafe timed safe**
https://www.thekitchensafe.com/

I use mine at least once a week. Once you get one you will see why.

Appendix one

Terminology

You may have noticed that in this book I was not consistent in the adjectives that I used to describe both the disease and the gambler. I've used "compulsive", "problem", "disordered", and "addicted" at various times in the book. Though, by the last half of the book I tended to use only "addicted" - i.e. "addicted gambler" to describe the person, and "gambling addiction" to describe the disease. What follows are some thoughts on each of the terms currently being used.

Pathological

Pathological is used to describe the person, but not usually the disease. Pathological was prominent over a decade ago but is now completely out of favor. Obviously, "pathological" is an unnecessarily negative term. It also doesn't really describe what is going on with the addiction. You wouldn't call the garden variety alcoholic a pathological drinker. This term should stay in the past.

Compulsive

Also used mostly to describe the person. While not as negative as pathological, it still doesn't quite capture the nature of the addiction. It looks like it is also currently out of favor.

GA still uses "compulsive gambler" in their literature and at meetings: "Hi, I'm Kurt, and I'm a compulsive gambler". As mentioned before, it is very difficult and expensive for GA to update their materials, so I assume "compulsive" will live on for some time at GA.

Problem

This is still in use at various sites and in the literature. The problem I have with "problem" is that it has become a little hazy. In some places it's used to describe a broad range of gamblers from those who gamble a little too much (and may be on the path to addiction) to those who are clearly addicted. Often when reading about gambling you don't know which group or groups they are referring to when they use "problem gambling".

The National Council on Problem Gaming (NCPG) continues to use "problem" since it its actually part of their name. I'm guessing they are stuck with it from now on.

Disordered

This is the hot up-and-comer in the world of gambling terminology. Used both for the person – "disordered gambler", and for the disease – "gambling disorder". The DSM-5 uses it (almost) exclusively. (Unfortunately, the DSM-5 slipped up once in the gambling disorder section and used the term "pathological gambling" when referring to the prevalence of gambling among African Americans.)

The National Center for Responsible Gaming (NCRG) website has completely converted to the "disordered" terminology in its website and literature.

For me, as a regular person and a non-professional, I don't like the "disordered" term at all. I don't think of myself as being disordered – what does that mean? And when I think of the term for the disease, "disordered gambling", I'm also confused. The picture I have in my mind of disordered gambling is a person wandering around the casino, confused, randomly placing bets, not understanding what they are doing. When I'm at a casino, I feel like my gambling is completely ordered.

Addicted

I prefer addicted or addiction: "Hi, I'm Kurt, and I'm addicted to gambling". To me "addicted" is the most accurate, and the most descriptive. Gambling addiction was only recently (2013) added to the section in the DSM-5 that includes things like drug and alcohol addiction. It is the only behavioral disorder included in this section with all the substance abuse disorders. That is good progress in the understanding that gambling is a true addiction and has many of the same characteristics as stimulant addiction.

Though in reading the entire DSM-5 section on all substance abuse disorders (addictions) I only find the term addiction once – and that is in the title of the section. For some reason that I'm not aware of, the DSM people are avoiding using the term "addiction" for anything. Of course, they are way smarter than I am about these things, so I'm sure they have a good reason.

Still, call me old fashioned, but I prefer addiction. I think it is time that we call it like it is. We are addicted to gambling. By being straight-up with it, others will now read and hear the term in the context of gambling and then perhaps start to understand what we are dealing with. We are addicted to gambling. Let it be known.

Appendix 2

Connecting the dots to determine the annual number of gambling caused suicides

Dot 1 - Total addicted gamblers in the United States

How many problem (pathological, addicted, disordered…take your pick) gamblers are there in the United States now? Unfortunately, there is not a clear number that can be quoted with much confidence. I've spent many hours reading surveys and studies. These studies and surveys use different methods and different criteria for determining the level of gambling disorder, and the results vary by factors of five or more.

There are at least three different criteria used to determine if the person was a problem/compulsive/severe gambler. The studies differ by the number of people asked, and most importantly, they vary by what year they were taken. Many were taken in the 1990's, well before the explosion of casinos and slot machines. However, they all identify one common trend – they almost always indicate that current year prevalence (meaning the year the survey was taken) is significantly higher than previous year's prevalence. In other words, addicted gambling is measurably on the rise.

If this was true in the 1990's, it is certainly increasing twenty years later, as these twenty years have seen a hundred fold increase in casinos and slot machines!

The NCRG (the industry group) states: "Approximately 1 percent of the adult population in the United States (the adult population of the U.S. is 250 million) has a severe gambling problem." Citing studies from 2008 and 1999. Once again, these studies are outdated.

The National Institutes of Health (NIH) meta-analysis (combining all relevant surveys and studies) puts the current year number of Level-3 (severe) disordered gamblers at 1.6% (and again, many of these studies were from the 1980s and 1990s).

An exhaustive Harvard Medical school meta-analysis pegs current year adult prevalence of level-3 gambling disorder at between 1.12% and 1.29%. This study was done in 1999! This is well before the explosion of casinos and slot machines.

There is no question that many more people are now addicted because of the radical increase in the local availability of casino gambling. And yet there seems to be no current studies that capture both the increase in casinos and the dramatic increase in the sophistication of current slot machines.

The DSM-5 puts the current year prevalence for disordered gambling at .2%-.3%. They cite no surveys, studies or sources to justify this claim. I'm not a fan of the DSM-5's four pages of description of disordered gambling. They make several outrageous and unsubstantiated claims. For example, they claim (two different times) that disordered gamblers are in poor health. Huh? In my experience at inpatient treatment, GA meetings, in the casino in general, and in discussions with therapists, I've not seen or heard anyone support that claim. My experience is that addicted gamblers look very much like a slice of the public at large. Many of the DSM-5 pronouncements seem to me to be grossly out of date. In any case, the DSM-5's data is, *in my opinion*, not remotely credible.

I believe a conservative middle ground for the prevalence percentage of addicted gamblers in the current environment of the year 2020 (considering that there are significantly more addicted gamblers now than there were ten and twenty years ago when most of the surveys were taken) is 2.0%.

(It is also important to note that suicides might occur in people who have very recently started gambling. Addiction can happen fast, especially with slot machines.)

Dot 2 - Annual attempted suicides by addicted gamblers

In the United States, a report by the National Council on Problem Gaming indicated that one in five pathological gamblers attempts suicide. It is also stated many other times in many other places that one out of five addicted gamblers have attempted suicide (note: an attempted suicide does not have to result in injury, so my high-speed search for a bridge abutment does count as an attempt).

However, this number of attempted suicides does not give us the number of attempted suicides *this year*. It means that one in five have attempted suicide during their entire gambling experience. There is absolutely no data available to tell us the addicted gambler *current year* attempted suicides. Again, I will offer an informed guess.

The number of people becoming addicted to gambling in any form is clearly on the rise. It is obvious that newly addicted gamblers (those becoming addicted in the last year), outnumber those gamblers who became un-addicted or died in the last year. I believe that differential is quite large. And that process of adding the newly addicted has been going on for many years and is accelerating (I can think of no reason why it would be decelerating).

So, I will propose that a reasonable number of last year's addicted gambler suicide attempts is 2%. That equates to one out of ten of the 20% of addicted gamblers who *have* attempted suicide at some point. I think this number passes the sniff test.

Dot 3 – The ratio of attempted suicides to completed (fatal) suicides for the general population.

In the U.S., the National Institute for Mental Health (NIMH) reports there are 11 nonfatal suicide attempts for every suicide death. The American Association of Suicidology reports higher numbers, stating that there are 25 suicide attempts for every suicide completion.

The data for this ratio is for the general public, and not just for addicted gamblers. So, these ratios include a significant number of "call-for-help" suicide attempts that are recorded each year. My belief is that among addicted gamblers, there are very few call-for-help type suicide attempts.

Addicted gamblers want their addiction to be secret. Often, the suicide has the specific purpose of getting insurance money for their family. I believe when they decide that suicide is the only way out, they are committed to doing it. For the committed suicidal addicted gambler, this ratio is probably closer to 5 to 1. To be conservative again, for the purpose of this exercise I'll propose a ratio of 8 to 1.

The equation:

We now have all the numbers we need to calculate annual addicted gambler completed suicides.

Total-addicted-gamblers (250 million (the number of adults in the United States)) X (2.0%) = 5,000,000

Annual suicide attempts   (5,000,000) X (2%) = 100,000

Annual completed suicides (100,000) / (8) = **12,500**

By this method, annual addicted gambler suicides are somewhere around 12,500. I believe my numbers are conservative, and not surprisingly, they yield a reasonable result.

Another path to determining the number of annual gambling-related suicides

Call this the commonsense approach. Once again, I will speak here only of slot machine addicted gamblers. Using the 2.0% prevalence figure, I claimed there were 5 million addicted gamblers. It is now commonly accepted that 60% to 80% of addicted gamblers are addicted to slot machines.

(I believe those percentages are a bit low for slot machine addicts. One only needs to go to any casino, and it is obvious that over 90% of the players at any time of the day are perched on a stool with a borg-like focus on their slot machine only inches away from their brain. Several casinos over the last few years have simply removed the table-games and replaced them with slot machines in order to maximize their financial return-per-square-foot of limited floor space.)

So, let's say that 70% of addicted gamblers are slot machine players – or 3,500,000 addicted slot players. There are currently between 1,000 and 2,000 casinos in some form of operation in this country. They range from the mega-casinos that have well over 5,000 slot machines to smaller casinos (like those in Montana and Oregon) that have only a few dozen machines. The best information available right now (though already probably out of date) is that there are more than 1,000,000 slot machines in the United States.

If you stood outside an average size casino on any day and watched the people leave, how many people per day would you guess walk out, with their head down, looking depressed or distraught, and slowly head to their car? These are the people that once again lost more money than they could afford. I've been part of that parade too many times to count. Every minute there are a handful leaving in that condition, every hour over a hundred, every day well over a thousand.

That's a million (a thousand casinos, times a thousand distraught people) seriously distressed people walking out of casinos every day! Let's say for the sake of this exercise that of those million seriously distressed people, just 5% are now suicidal, that only one out of twenty are thinking that suicide might be an option, Now we are talking about 50,000 people (every day!) considering suicide. Of course, almost all will reject even making a suicide attempt.

But what if just 1% of that 50,000 potentially suicidal people follow through and decide to kill themselves. Now we have 500 people on the path of committing suicide. And now what if only 10% of these people *do kill themselves*? That's 50 suicides every day, or *18,250 suicides per year!*

Is any of what I speculated about above that hard to believe? Is it hard to believe that out of 1,000,000 distraught people leaving the casino having lost a good deal of money, that out of those million people, those with their brain chemistry compromised by extended slot machine torture, that those fundamentally impulsive people wondering why they can't stop, is it hard to believe that 50 of them would chose to escape by killing themselves?

I would say it is harder to believe why there aren't more (and my guess is that there are more).

Of course, this commonsense approach is not science. But it is a reasonable thought experiment, I think it passes the sniff test, and the conclusion is completely in line with the proposed gambling-related suicide deaths arrived at by other methods.

One last thought

From a book by June Hunt: *Gambling Your Life Away,* 2013

"In Gulfport Mississippi, suicides increased by 213 percent (from 24 to 75) in the first two years after casinos arrived. In neighboring Biloxi, suicide attempts jumped by 1,000 percent (from 6 to 66) in the first year alone."

Acknowledgements

It is my good fortune that five expert professionals agreed to read my manuscript and offer feedback.

Devonna Rowlette, a certified Washington State gambling therapist, and Maureen Greely, the Director of Washington State's Evergreen Council on Problem Gambling, were both early readers and offered many helpful ideas.

Sheryl Anderson, the Director of Vanguard Center for Gambling Recovery at Project Turnabout, has provided me an incredible amount of detailed analysis, helpful suggestions, and positive support from the beginning to the end of this project. I could not be more thankful for her amazing contributions.

Keith Whyte, the Executive Director of the National Council on Problem Gambling (NCPG) read the final manuscript and offered several excellent suggestions that led to positive changes in this published version of the book.

Douglas G Smith, former co-founder of Y.E.S. (Youth Emergency Services, one of the nation's first call-in crisis helplines) and a long time great friend, read the manuscript and weighed in positively on this book's unusual concept of preparing ahead of time for an unanticipated existential crisis.

It was also my good luck to have two copy editors help me convert my fractured prose into something acceptable. My long-time friend Jonathan McCormick slogged through my mess and wore out his red marker. Jon is as good a wordsmith as anyone I have ever known. Last, but definitely not least, my eldest son Oscar Dahl (an excellent writer) likewise used up his red ink and then coordinated the merging of his and Jon's multitude of corrections. In this effort, Oscar received a heavy dose of his father's addiction and imperfections. Once again my good fortune held, as he continues to speak to me and is often quite nice about it.

I want to give thanks to the Vanguard Center for Gambling Recovery. I am a proud alumnus. The counseling I received there was first-rate, the facility amenities and food were also excellent. But what I will always remember are the other recovering addicted gamblers that I met and got to know so well in such a short time. A thirty-day inpatient treatment becomes an unexpectedly intimate event. I hope that they are all succeeding in their recovery. And I hope the same for you!

About the Author

Mr. Dahl's writing career began with a weekly column in the Sunday Seattle Times newspaper (500k circ.) called 2020world. The column (and its associated on-line component) could legitimately claim to be one of the world's first blogs. Steve Case, Bill Gates, and other technology luminaries were among the over ten thousand online readers and participants (this was in 1993, before the World Wide Web had emerged).

He moved on to study and write about our looming sustainability crisis. Many of his essays have been published on respected internet sites that focus on sustainability, overpopulation, and the potential for a dangerous outcome to our unabated growth.

He has written two novels. The Eden Proposition, completed in 2009, received solid acclaim, excellent reviews, and several self-published awards. His second novel, a speculative fiction thriller titled "An American Famine" is also available on Amazon.

Mr. Dahl currently resides in the-middle-of-nowhere, southwest Washington State with a Golden Retriever that is known locally as a stable genius.

Made in United States
Troutdale, OR
11/20/2023

14758602R10135